# GETTING THEM SOBER

## VOLUME

# 4

## Separation Decisions

### Toby Rice Drews

RECOVERY COMMUNICATIONS, INC.
P.O. Box 19910 • Baltimore, Maryland 21211 • (410) 243-8558

*This book is dedicated to those people I love and from whom I continue to learn:*
*Liz Brandt; Sue Brown; Bob Kent; Ron Lawson; Claire Murphy; Jim Muth; Adele Rice Nudel, my sister*

## Other Books By Toby Rice Drews:

Getting Them Sober, Volume 1
Getting Them Sober, Volume 2
Getting Them Sober, Volume 3
Getting Your Children Sober
Get Rid of Anxiety and Stress
Sex and the Sober Alcoholic
Light This Day

*To order these books, and for further information about Toby Rice Drews' audio- and video-cassettes, please see back pages, under "Resources."*

The information printed herein is not intended to be considered counseling or other professional advice by the publisher, author, or contributors. The publisher and author are not responsible for the outcome of services provided by those parties whose advertisements appear in this book.

Book design by Belle Vista Graphics
Copyright © 1992 by Toby Rice Drews
All rights reserved.   Printed in the United States of America
Library of Congress Catalog Card Number: 85-73330
International Standard Book Number: 0-9615995-1-0

# Contents

# Author's Introduction

If we're in a relationship with an alcoholic, we think about leaving — for an hour, for a day, or forever.

When we do think about leaving, our decision-making powers get "muddied up" by other issues. For instance, we spend hours wondering "if we did enough," or "if we hadn't done such and such, would it be different?" We spend even more time obsessing about what they're doing and how to stop them. Not that it isn't human to do this, but the problem is, we can't stop ourselves from obsessing — even when we want to.

We run into strangers, who, in the course of just exchanging small-talk, say things that we attach great meanings to, and that make us feel crazy. (For instance: a woman met another woman at a bus-stop on the way to work, and the second woman talked about her "wonderful children." The first woman's kids were all abusive alcoholics, but she immediately started feeling guilty for being angry at her children and not believing that her kids, too, were "wonderful.")

These and other issues prevent us from clearheadedly seeing our situations. They stop us from being focused on what is *really* wrong. They provide a totally unbalanced view of ourselves and others. They make us see ourselves as always guilty, no matter what we do or choose. They put us in a no-win situation.

In Part One of this book, these illusions are identified and exposed for what they are, to help you get out from under the alcoholic's craziness. *This is of utmost importance for your sanity and growth, whether or not you stay with, or leave, the alcoholic.*

\* \* \*

Even when we know what we want to do, we often have little self-trust in order to be able to *stay* with our decisions.

Often, we really want to stay with the alcoholic. For now, anyway.

But we rightfully want to leave open the door to all the options — including leaving.

Many times, we try to leave and we get frightened about being alone; or lonesome (which is different from fearful of being alone); or anxious about change; or worried about the alcoholic. And we go back, even more depressed than ever. (*How* did it happen?)

Maybe we've left and stayed away, and wound up in a relationship with yet another emotionally-unavailable person. We think that "It'll always be that way for me."

Part Two of the book helps with those issues. It will see you through much of the usual family-of-the-alcoholic vacillations that we all go through. It will help you to more easily decide what you *really* want to do — and help you to reach a calmer state of mind about your decision.

\* \* \*

Part Three of the book will help you to avoid listening to advice-givers who are guilt-makers and help you to stop believing them as if they have the gospel! It will teach you how to discern who *really* knows what they are talking about, when they give you advice about your alcoholic relationship.

\* \* \*

Part Four will lead you literally by the hand through all the "what-ifs" you will probably go through, should you decide to separate. It exposes the myths that have confused families and that have needlessly sent them back into abusive situations.

\* \* \*

This book is about:

*Why* we are so attached to them

How to make a decision whether to stay or leave

How to understand that you have the ethical right to leave a bad situation, *even if you choose not to do so*

Whom to trust about advice

How to trust your own decisions about staying or leaving, and stop questioning/torturing yourself (i.e., "He says he's drinking less since we separated . . . *was* it my fault?" or "But he looks so good, now; maybe I was wrong; maybe he's not an alcoholic and I should have stayed?")

If we've chosen to separate, is there hope for a good future for us — despite all our emotional baggage from living with craziness (and adapting to it) all those years?

* * *

There is also an important special section: an interview with David Evans, Chair of the Alcoholism and Drug Law Reform Committee of the Individual Rights and Responsibilities Section of the American Bar Association.

Evans answers the legal questions you called and wrote to me about: how to protect your children if you're separated and the non-custodial parent picks them up while driving drunk; how to choose the right attorney; court-ordered evaluations for alcoholics; and much more.

There is also an interview with Robert White, President of the Maryland Chapter of the National Council on Alcoholism and Drug Dependence. Rob has been a professional interventionist for eleven years. He gives new insight into the value of interventions — for the *family* as well as the alcoholic/addict. He also tells how the spouse can avoid being the "heavy" in that situation.

* * *

This book is also for your attorney.

He gets angry because he doesn't understand: (a) why you drop the proceedings and (b) why it seems that what you say about your alcoholic spouse appears too bizarre to believe (actually, you're probably understating the case!).

What your lawyer doesn't know is that you vacillate because of terror. That you do whatever you do, *not* because you want to be contrary or perverse . . . but because your head is spinning, after living with that alcoholic.

*And your attorneys would very likely act the same way with their own attorneys, if they were separating from drinking alcoholics!*

This book is for the attorney who is charmed by the alcoholic adversary, and thinks his own client — the spouse — is "over-reactive."

And, lastly but very importantly, this book is meant to enlighten judges who do not understand how alcoholism subtly distorts testimony and evidence — often resulting in further harm to families, particularly the children.

– 3 –

# Part One:
## What Are The Illusions That We Believe, That Keep Us So Attached To Alcoholic/ Abusive/Unavailable People?

# Chapter One:
## Everybody Blames The Family

"Blame" can be very attaching. What does that mean? It means that family members who get blamed by the alcoholic (and doesn't *that* happen frequently?!) spend an enormous amount of time trying to defend themselves or beating themselves up, emotionally.

This time spent gets the family more embroiled with the alcoholic — more emotionally attached. This is the opposite of recovery, which is "emotional detachment" from the craziness of living with an alcoholic.

The problem gets compounded when not only the alcoholic blames the family ("I wouldn't drink if you wouldn't nag . . . "), but when counselors join in that blame, with: "I think he's maybe not an alcoholic, Mrs. Jones; perhaps he just drinks because the atmosphere in the house is so grim. Perhaps you can learn to be a happier person and communicate with him better, and then he'll not drink as much?" Families go through this kind of abuse from counselors all too frequently.

When the alcoholic and the counselor join together to blame the family for the alcoholic's alcoholism, the family often gets confused and blames themselves, also. (They say things to themselves, like, "Maybe if I baked him seven peach pies instead of seven apple pies, he'd be okay and not drink.")

Families spend much time trying to figure out where they went wrong. Then they attempt to "rectify" things so "he'd be happy" (when you really can't please an alcoholic). Or they take in the blame and try to defend themselves.

All this results in much *more* attachment to the alcoholic's craziness.

\* \* \*

What can help?

Just remembering the facts:

a) That "blame," and irrational family guilt resulting from the blame, is part and parcel of the disease. When you begin to dissect every little nuance that the alcoholic says (to see if there is any truth in it, so that you can find the way to see where you went wrong and said things to "make him drink") — immediately tell yourself that it is the disease talking and you will *not* pay any more attention to it!

b) If you're living with an alcoholic and if you've been blamed by counselors for "the atmosphere in the home" or "over-reacting" or "inappropriate rage" — remember that many counselors who say they understand alcoholism actually do not. Many counselors are themselves adult children of alcoholics who have not been treated for their own denial systems (in them since birth), and therefore cannot truly see the disease. Or, they may still have their own untreated rage at their non-addicted parent and that often spills over into the professional counseling situation — without their even knowing it.

c) Attending Al-Anon will help you to get detachment from the nuttiness and teach you self-trust. With that gift of self-trust, no alcoholic, no counselor, can ever keep you in dis-ease again.

# Chapter Two:
## Don't Try To Make Sense Out Of Their Nonsense

One of the ways we get pulled into feeling crazy again is when they say something that is totally nonsensical and abusive about us—and then imply that we are crazy if we don't agree with them.

A case in point: Ron was married three years to Cheryl. When he was ready to go off on a drunk, she'd know it about four days before it was about to happen. He'd get "that look of nuttiness in his eyes." Then, he'd start on a roll.

He'd begin by making little cracks to her. When she protested that she didn't care for his remarks, he told her she didn't have a "sense of humor." That she was too "sensitive."

Then would follow his totally off-the-wall comments about how badly she conducted areas of her life where she *knew* she did well. But, by the time he finished, her head would be in a whirl. She found herself defending the things she'd done for years that were effective, as if she had made mountains of mistakes.

For instance, Cheryl worked in real estate. She was very good at it. Most of their income was from her rentals. Ron was virtually unemployable by this time, just doing temporary manual labor when he could get it. Cheryl paid the bills.

When he would "start his stuff," he'd question her ability to make sound real-estate buying decisions . . . even though he'd never done it!

When he started bad-mouthing her, Cheryl would get a gut reaction of fear and question her professional decisions, even though she had always trusted herself before he began all this. Then, after she saw what he was doing, she became understandably very angry, and told him how he was living off her and had no knowledge of real estate, and how dare he!

Instead of responding to the issue, Ron would accuse her of "always throwing it in his face that she made more money."

Then, Cheryl tried to show him how she had a right to answer him that way, since he had said what he said.

Of course, he never answered her directly. He just went on with his crazymaking: "You're paranoid. I never attacked you. You always think everyone's always attacking you."

She: "Isn't it funny that it's always you who attacks me! And I never think anyone else is doing that!"

He stops. Goes on to what he was doing (watching t.v. and drinking beer) and gets anesthetized.

She is exhausted, furious, and wonders how she got sucked into it again.

\* \* \*

What did Cheryl do to turn it around and get out from under his power over her?

a) She worked hard to internalize the fact that he really *did* understand the truth — he just wanted to get under her skin. There was no need for her to "show him" the truth.

b) Besides that, and more importantly — she came to believe that he truly wasn't a tin-god to her anymore. That if he chose to try to belittle her, he certainly did not deserve a title role in her life!

c) Once she began to really believe the above two statements, she began to look beyond him for validation and companionship. She once more surrounded herself with good friends and outward, joyous activities that enhanced her — things she used to do before getting so entrapped with an alcoholic.

d) As her world widened, she went from being with anyone who would have the time to be with her (as she found she had to do, at first) to choosing to be with people who were inherently excited by life, not just "safe." She used to choose people to be with who had lots of problems because it made her feel good that she had fewer ones. However, she began to see that there were several downsides to that. One was that their persona was basically negative. She found herself slowly cloaked with negativity, even though it gave her a temporary good feeling. Furthermore, she could not begin to see all the wonderful options open to her when she chose to be surrounded by small-minded negativists. For, pessimism is catching. It very, very subtly erodes the soul. She began to choose friends who spoke more of their expanding universes rather than their problems. They were into transcending problems and living in their joys, not their sorrows — and she caught the bug! She grew from survival to enhancement!

Once this happened to her, even with setbacks, she never again lived totally within her alcoholic's negative universe.

## Chapter Three:
## Knowing That It's Hard To Lose An Alcoholic, Helps To Calm Us Down And Keep Us On The Recovery Path

I said in my first book, *Getting Them Sober, Volume One,* that it's hard to lose an alcoholic. People have written to me and asked me what I meant by that.

Basically, it means this: You can marry him; divorce him; remarry someone else; repeat the process. And the *probability* is that he'll *still* want to be with you (whatever that means to him), in the long run.

I know of a couple who have been separated for over 40 years. He lives in the woods of New Hampshire as a resident alcoholic recluse. Each Christmas, Easter, and birthday, he sends her a card . . . and he still considers her "his wife."

This is not unusual.

This can be useful information to have, to get through the times when you are feeling panicky about losing him.

However, you may ask, "But *when* will he come back, this time?"

It seems unfortunate, but the alcoholic/addict often begins to return home (wooing you all over again, albeit for a short time before starting on his "junk" again) *when you begin to not want him around anymore.*

He often appears again *before* you get over him entirely (and you can!). He probably doesn't want to lose you. He has what I call "alcoholic radar." (When they are into this behavior, they know just what to do; when to pop up).

During those terrible panic times when you are unable to do much else than think about getting him back, it can be very comforting to have this information. And it helps to know that even if he leaves again, if you are willing to put up with it, he probably will keep coming back.

But, it is good to *remember the facts:* as long as he continues to drink, the alcoholic will probably continue his elusive behavior.

Remembering that can help you to become more self-protective and keep some of yourself emotionally separated from the situation.

Later, when you are calmer, you can deal with the idea of staying in a relationship with an alcoholic (or otherwise emotionally-unavailable person).

But, for now, just knowing that he will most likely be back (if you still want him) can help you through these panic-times.

*　*　*

Counselors sometimes ask me, "Why do you reassure her that he'll probably come back, when it's healthier for her to realize how sick that relationship is, and that she must let go?"

When families enter treatment, they most likely do not have to be told that an abusive (emotionally and/or physically) relationship is not good for them. They know it.

Very often, her history is that she and the alcoholic have both blamed her for the relationship problems over the years. If I chastise her for wanting him back, I am subtly adding to that blame to make her feel, again, that she is "wrong."

If a counselor is baffled and shocked by the fact that she "still wants him back," she does not understand addictive families.

Families' greatest fear is that "they will lose him."

Only if we can get beyond that obsessive fear, by telling her the reassuring facts, can we seriously get down to looking at options. For, when her panic dies down, she is often very willing to begin to look at reality. If I press her to look at this reality too soon, she will probably stop treatment, and then there is no chance to help her.

In other words, we do not lose ground by not getting right down to Divorce and Getting On With Your Life. And if I focus on what I think she should do (instead of understanding that she is nowhere near that, in reality), she inherently knows that I know nothing about her.

# Chapter Four:
# The Irregular Behavior Of The Alcoholic Keeps Us Attached

When an alcoholic gives us comfort and love on an irregular basis — when we cannot know when he or she will be nice — we are much more bound to them than if they gave us love on a regular basis.

The reason for this strong bonding with someone who gives love inconsistently is that, since we want the love, we are anxiously awaiting it.

*Therefore, we pay a lot of attention to him, watching out for when he might be loving. All this "paying a lot of attention" bonds us very tightly to the object or person to whom we are paying so much attention. This "closeness" is not necessarily "love." It is often more of a bonding due to that intensity, mistaking it for "a close relationship."*

We do not have to pay such close attention at all to the person who comes home at 6 p.m., is nice, says hello, reads the paper, helps with dinner and cleanup, watches t.v., and goes to bed. We know the outcome of our interacting with him; it's normal. We expect the kindness; we get it regularly. We have no need to spend any time looking for it.

That's probably why, in healthy families, people seem "less close" than they do in alcoholic families.

So, when you berate yourself for "being *so* attached," remember that much of that attachment is not "your fault."

And, even though you've been programmed to respond in a super-attentive way to the alcoholism, just *knowing* that can help you to begin to detach from the sickening effects of an alcoholic on your life.

\* \* \*

And, if you are dating, please don't worry that you will "turn" a nice relationship into a sick one (because of past patterns). If we pick decent people to be with, we can't "turn" them into indecent people. If we act in old, anxious ways, and if we are in self-help groups or counseling to end destructive patterns, nice people are patient with us, have compassion for us, and give us time to heal.

# Chapter Five:
# The Alcoholic Does Not Exist
# Separately From The Alcoholism

I hear a lot from family members that they "can't totally believe that the alcoholism has that much control over the alcoholic."

Very often, that statement stems from a belief system that tells the family that "there's the alcoholism over *here* — and the alcoholic and his nuttiness over *there.*"

They think of alcoholism only as: cirrhosis of the liver, or late-stage brain damage, or falling-down drunkenness.

They can't quite believe that the alcoholism controls all the person's thoughts, actions, and feelings.

Why is the family unable to get past their own denial?

a) The family doesn't really understand that a person's thoughts, feelings, and actions are highly influenced by toxic poisons acting on the brain/spinal cord/central nervous system.

The alcohol isn't just working on the brain when the person is drinking. It takes a long time to get it out of the system, and the alcoholic is usually drinking again before it's out. So, there isn't usually any real "sobriety" at all.

(Picture people going into surgery with "twilight drugs." They say weird things and are not "loving and understanding and involved with their spouses." Picture doing this for months and years, day after day, and you have regularly-distorted thoughts, feelings, and actions.)

b) The family often wants to believe that there really is a psychiatric reason for all this. This is because if the alcoholic refuses to go to treatment, the family naturally feels despairing and hopes that the problem may be something *other* than the alcoholism — so that the alcoholic will go to *some* kind of "treatment." (In the hope that *something* "will take" and he'll get well.)

The problem is, the majority of therapists do not understand alcoholism. They often try to help the alcoholic focus on his/her childhood to supposedly "get to the root of the problem." They think that the "root of the problem" is *not alcoholism*, but a psychiatric reason. They believe, therefore, that the alcoholic can't really stop drinking until that "psychiatric root cause" is found. Then (according to this theory), the real need for alcoholic drinking would just wither away.

The alcoholic often agrees to go to this kind of treatment because he knows it leaves his drinking intact.

The problem is, that treatment approach seldom works.

Alcoholism is *not* secondary to a psychiatric problem. Alcoholism is a primary disease in and of itself.

Historically, millions of alcoholics have died from the effects of alcoholic drinking — while trying to "get at the root of the problem" in therapy. (As a matter of fact, many people *do* discover, and "work on," their childhood trauma in therapy — and *still* continue to drink and die.)

And, even if there *is* a psychiatric problem in *addition* to the alcoholism, it is very difficult to treat the mental illness unless total abstinence from alcohol is first attained.

It is also extremely difficult to even diagnose whether or not a person has a psychiatric illness in addition to alcoholism, if that person is still drinking. The alcohol-induced crazy behavior must be at least somewhat abated by sobriety, in order to correctly assess the patient. (Many people have been incorrectly diagnosed as "mentally ill" — when in fact they have *alcohol-induced* behaviors that mimic mental illness.)

Additionally, it is often difficult to convince an alcoholic to leave ineffective psychiatric counseling — to go for real help for the alcoholism — because that attendance at the therapist's office is a further excuse to continue drinking! The alcoholic says to the family, "What do you mean, get help? I'm getting help! I've been seeing my therapist every week now for five years! What more do you want?" And sadly, many therapists who do not understand alcoholism, really believe that the "family interaction" causes the alcoholic's drinking. Therefore, those therapists focus *not* on the alcoholism, but on the "family anger" at the alcoholic. As a result, more blaming of the family goes on — this time with the stamp of approval of therapy.

c) The family sees the alcoholic as such a tin-god — so powerful — they wind up with a block against believing that anything is more powerful than the alcoholic. (The alcoholic has told the family that for years, and the family naturally believes it.)

* * *

Think about how powerful you think your alcoholic is. Think about how it colors all your beliefs about control issues; about treatment; about what you have the right to do and not to do; and about your self-image.

* * *

Read the chapter on Intervention with the idea in mind that you are not as much under the alcoholic's thumb as you think you are — and the alcoholic is certainly not as powerful as you think he/she is.

And please don't read the chapter and then put yourself down if you're not wanting to do an intervention, or are not ready for it. It's just another option.

# Chapter Six:
## Excited Misery Keeps Us Attached To The Alcoholic

Caroline was talking with me from her home in San Francisco. She grew up in Chicago and moved to California when she was in her early teens. She had married at 18 and had two children by the time she reached 21.

"I was so unworldly. I went from growing up in an alcoholic home, to marrying my first husband. He was very religious, worked 11 hours a day, and was a good man and very steady — and very boring.

"He was very good to me. But I wasn't ready for that. I wasn't treated for the effects that growing up in an alcoholic home had on me.

"What I mean was, I was used to the up-and-down excitement that happened all the time, at home. And then I married very young, this normal man! It was like being buried! So *nothing*. Evenness. I knew nothing about it; I wasn't *used* to it. It was like I was looking around, uneasily, for something to make something happen!

"Then, I met Wayne. He worked where I was working. He was always chattering, always going in and out of the office, always on the move. He talked with me about things I loved; he talked incessantly! I didn't realize he talked so much, so obsessively, because of the alcohol in his system. I just wanted constant anything; especially constant talking. My husband didn't talk that much. He just worked and went to church and ate and rested and did everything very on time and very predictably. Very normal. You could set your clock by him.

"But, Wayne was exciting! He came on like gangbusters. He swept me off my feet. Absolutely as charming as he could be. I would find little gifts in my desk drawer.

"But there was that side of him (like with a lot of alcoholics) that wanted me to be not only exciting, but the madonna. He loved the fact that I was also a devout Catholic, and he thought I was very humble.

"He was *so* attentive, at first, that it startled me. For instance, I would mention this record I loved, and it would be on my desk the next day.

"I was falling in love with him. I felt so guilty when I began to realize that. So, I went to my priest. And I said to him, 'Father, I'm sure I have committed adultery, because of what's in my mind.'

"And the priest said, 'Don't worry about it. Talk about something else with him. Like the weather. Things like that.'

"What a naive, young priest. What a naive, young *me!* I actually believed it might work! Of course, I tried it once, and it did no good."

\* \* \*

What I find so sad is that young people who grow up in alcoholic families invariably say to me, "I've left all that behind me. I don't need any help. It's history."

The *patterns* we carry with us!

They attach us to sick situations. They attach us to the wrong people. They attach us to excited misery.

And that need for "excitement" comes in many packages: Exciting jobs (like the young woman who only can "enjoy" high-stress work situations and mountain-climbing vacations. All this after her doctor told her it was dangerous for her heart.)

Or, hours spent each day on the phone with friends, discussing the horrors of illness or who-did-what-to-whom.

Or, hanging out where things are "happening." Liking — needing — the "atmosphere." Feeling empty when you can't get there for a couple of evenings.

Telling oneself that "everyone would like this way of life." When it isn't so.

Just becoming aware of these feelings, these needs, these patterns — this can be life-changing. When we don't know that this is essentially harmful to us, that this derives from alcoholic family patterns, we go along blindly and continue with no self-direction.

We remain attached to a way of life that is never satisfying, never contents us for more than an hour or so. And then, we need more.

That subconscious attachment-need for "excitement" keeps

many a family member in an alcoholic marriage.

We sometimes think, "I can leave financially; I have no trouble living alone. Why am I still here?"

We cannot extricate ourselves from *any* pattern until we begin to see it.

# Chapter Seven:
# Our Need To Caretake Keeps Us Involved With The Sickness

Caroline is a physician's assistant in Wyoming. An independent, short, bouncy woman who raised five children, Caroline was married to two alcoholics. She tells me it's "no accident that she is in the medical profession."

"I was terribly needy, and at the same time, I had this big need to take care of others. Both sides. Both extremes.

"I never felt that I had ever finished my work. I still go home and call in to check on patients. I do that about three times a week. And the other people on duty at night will tell me, 'Caroline, will you quit calling in!' Or they'd say, 'Just let it go!'

"I find it very difficult to quit worrying. I'm living alone, now. And work is a big part of my life."

I asked her if it was really that work is such a big issue or is it that this is a way to bring home the caretaking.

She thought about it. "Yeah, I think so. I mean, even when I'm grocery shopping — I can't go through a grocery line without helping someone. If I see a product that someone is looking at, I have to stop and help them choose!"

I said, "We adult children of alcoholics rush in where angels fear to tread!"

We both laughed.

\* \* \*

One suggestion that helped Caroline was: go into changing this pattern *slowly*. When we have a severe case of caretaking — one that is disrupting our lives to some degree — it is a good idea to very slowly extricate ourselves. For instance, if you've already helped one person in the supermarket, forego the urge to help another stranger pick out her food. If you've made one call to work to see if you are needed, try to postpone the second unnecessary call that day.

By doing this self-stopping slowly, you can avoid the anxiety that accompanies the guilt from cutting off of one's caretaking behavior. Of course, if you're completely sick and tired of it, and ready to end this needless behavior entirely, you're fortunate! But most people who've lived with alcoholism for any length of time, develop huge reserves of irrational guilt about not taking care of anyone and anybody.

How to be good to yourself:

a)  Become aware of your caretaking patterns.

b)  Become aware of their frequency and random targets.

c)  End the irrational caretaking slowly.

d)  Do not beat on yourself for having "done it for so many years."

e)  Tell yourself you will be a more effective person for when you are *really* needed if you are not continually depleted by irrational caretaking.

f)  Know that you will eventually change for yourself. You might begin by changing "to be a power of example" for your children. Know that that is okay.

# Chapter Eight:
## Facing Our Illusions — Ends Their Power To Hurt Us

"When I separated from my alcoholic husband, I couldn't move a stick of furniture. It was the way *he* liked it. It helped me believe I still had a marriage. Then, my therapist said that a rug and a chair don't make a marriage."

\* \* \*

When we are from alcoholic families, we are so used to illusion. We believe the alcoholic when (s)he says, "It'll be different."

When we are handed a crumb of decency, we say They Are Wonderful!

In order to stay in the relationship, we make worlds out of little good things that other people take for granted . . . because there is no regularity of goodness.

So, we accommodate more and more to fantasy, to illusion, to symbolism.

\* \* \*

Maryjo used to polish this little plate her husband won for her at a carnival. That event occurred eight years ago. It was a rare good night. He was nice to her for the whole evening.

That plate became very important.

\* \* \*

When the alcoholic is gone and we miss him, we substitute the plate and the rug and give those objects the power to comfort us. We give them the power to help us pretend that the relationship is good and still there. For awhile, that is comforting, and perhaps necessary. But after time passes, it becomes a bit of a reason for a depressed way of life.

And we don't even know it.

Don't other people with losses go through this? Yes. Are alcoholic families different? I believe so.

Because we are masters at self-deception about the alcoholism, we can transfer our denial to everything else so easily.

Other persons with losses recognize illusionary thinking, feel sad about it, and can usually eventually drop it.

For alcoholic families, this is much more traumatic. When *we* drop illusion, what is there left?

* * *

A client of mine tells me that the alcoholic man she was dating is now with another woman. She *intellectually* knows that this other woman isn't having fun with him, much of the time.

But, when she sees them together, in her mind's eye, she sees "The Donna Reed Show."

We are all so symbolic about everything in life, when we're from alcoholic families. We see a postcard about Christmas, and we feel that that is how life is supposed to be. And we assume that everyone lives that way — except us.

But, Christmas is only Norman Rockwell-wonderful when the people involved are nice to each other. If, instead, it's a typical alcoholic family, it's a zoo.

The symbolism is only as good as the application in each specific situation.

But, what we unconsciously tell ourselves is that if we plunk on the externals, then — zappo! — we've got everything okay! In other words, we believe that if we dress a certain way, send our kids to certain schools, have the correct credentials — then alcoholism is *not* supposed to disrupt our lives.

The problem is, the more we deny reality and dig our heels into believing that symbolism and fairy tales are the truth, the more devastated we are when reality finally does hit home.

* * *

Telling ourselves the truth about our situation — *even when we cannot leave it or change it much* — doesn't have to depress us.

For, when we are honest with ourselves, we expand our vision. We begin to *see* options. Therefore, we get hope.

And we are finally able to drop the anxious way of life that is the underpinning to illusion.

# Chapter Nine:
# Quick Ways To Detach

"Detaching" means: To emotionally separate yourself from the alcoholic, when he or she is hurtful to you. If you can detach at that time, you will not at all be as devastated by him as you had been, before. This not only emotionally protects you, but it also helps the alcoholic.

How? When *you* do not feel the effects of his acting-out disease, *he* will feel them. The alcoholic is only acting outward so that he won't feel his own inner pain. He "throws the pain outward" so that *he* cannot feel it.

But if it doesn't land on you, it has no effect. And if it doesn't land elsewhere, it comes back to him. One could say that it "boomerangs back onto him."

Only when they feel their own pain, will most alcoholics do anything about it.

*　*　*

Some tangible ways to detach (to disable the alcoholic's disease from hurting you):

☐ In your mind's eye: Draw a circle on the ground. Place your left foot in that circle and keep your right foot outside of that circle. Inside the circle is your relationship. You've only got one foot in it. You're only half-invested in it. You're more able to coolly observe the relationship that way, and not get so hurt by it.

☐ Name the left foot (that's in the circle) "Intellect." Name the right foot (that's outside the circle) "Emotions." You've kept your emotions out of the way of that circle of sickness, and protected yourself from the alcoholic's disorder.

☐ Picture yourself in a car with a stickshift. The stickshift controls the tone of your reaction to the relationship. Put it in neutral. The alcoholic cannot emotionally hurt you. Only you are at the controls.

☐ If the alcoholic is the type who gets to you by glaring at you, don't have eye contact when he's "on a roll." Look at his forehead, the wall, the window. He's not your father. You do not have to obey and look at him. You have dignity.

☐ Figuratively, take your hand and push his face away from you, when you can't see anything else in your mind but what he's doing. Now, you can begin to see *around* him. There's a big world out there that has nothing to do with what he's doing.

☐ Go to the library and see all the medical books on alcoholism. Spread them out on the table. Scan their information. Give yourself a few hours to do this. This will help you to believe it is a disease. Then, you can know, more, that the alcoholic is driven by something bigger than he or she is. It's as if they're programmed. It diminishes your feelings that "it's him that's so powerful."

# Part Two:
## Making The Decision

# Chapter Ten:
# "I Had To Stop Being
# So 'Strong' — So I Could
# Get The Help I Needed"

**JENINE:** "I really felt very, very strongly that, in the end, in any given situation, God would help me. And I have always turned to Him. And I have always asked for His strength.

"I sort of feel when you are begging the alcoholic to be nice, it's like it says in the Bible, something about casting your pearls before swine."

**TOBY:** "That sounds like alcoholism in a nutshell! When we financially support an alcoholic who is abusive, it's like we pawn the pearls to take care of the swine!"

**JENINE:** "Exactly! And when I realized that I am worthwhile, it was like a fleeting glimpse. You don't feel that way every day. There are days you feel rotten about yourself; you feel worse than that. You feel that you are not really worthy of anything, so you take everything that you have to take from that alcoholic, that day.

"But, once in a while, this little light comes on that says, 'You are worthwhile.' You have taken enough of this junk. You cannot demean yourself any longer. You have to get out of this situation because he is going to continue to do that to you.

"I was always embarrassed that I was taking it. I think that's when I realized one of the many things that helped push me out: that I was ashamed about where I had allowed myself to be pushed. At the level I had allowed myself to get to.

"You talk about an alcoholic allowing himself to get down to the gutter level from drinking. Well, I had allowed him to push *me* down into the gutter by his verbal abuse, his emotional abuse. He was never physically abusive, but the emotional and mental abuse was unbelievable.

"I had allowed him to send me into a really low ebb. When this suddenly dawned on me, then every day, in some small way, it would come up again. This revelation about how bad it really was.

"Have you heard of the Hound of Heaven? It's from Dante's *Divine Comedy*. God is called the Hound of Heaven. And He's not going to let you go if He wants you as His child.

"God is going to keep coming after you, no matter what you do.

"And I felt that. With all my friends and all my family reaching out to me — through them — God was working. Through them, He was the Hound of Heaven, coming after me.

"No matter what I did, He was going to make me face up to the fact that I was worthwhile. That I couldn't live any longer like this.

"I would look up and constantly think, 'the Hound of Heaven's after me.' I've got to make this decision. I've got to do this. I've got to have faith. I've got to have trust. I could no longer lie to myself. I could no longer demean myself. I had allowed Tim to do this. I can't do it to myself. Because God isn't going to let me. The Hound of Heaven wasn't going to let me.

"That was what really saved me, helped me, to pull out of that. About a week before my divorce became final, I was driving to work about 9 a.m. I would say my prayers in the morning, on the beltway. And I said to Him, 'Well, you know, God, this is finally finalized.' At one time, I never thought that this would happen. That I would be able to make this break. At least, legally. Whether I had done it emotionally or otherwise, yet, I wasn't sure.

"But I just never realized that when I was asking help from God, I could never ask for help from anyone else. I never asked them to do anything for me. I always felt it was an imposition. And I admired that about myself. I assumed it meant I was 'strong.' I always said, 'Oh, never mind. I'll be able to do that myself.' And they'd say, 'Are you sure?' And I'd always say, 'Sure!'

"If I asked anyone to help me, I really condemned myself. I'd be really angry that I had to ask them.

"I didn't know that I didn't feel worthy of their help.

"But I could always ask God. The trouble was, He was putting these people out there, to help me, and I kept rejecting them. I'd say to myself, 'I can't ask them to help me!' *I wanted God to do it. Not them.*

"I wanted that answer in some other way. I wanted Him to wrinkle His nose and make everything perfect. But I didn't want to go through other people. I would do the work, if He wanted. But I couldn't ask them to do the work. I felt that that was scut-work, helping me.

"Well, if I've learned anything, it's that other people are truly the instruments of God. They're His children, and I *had* to learn to accept His gifts.

"And you don't necessarily receive back from those you helped. You receive from others. That's the way it seemed to work for me.

"Suddenly, it's turned around. You're not the strong one. They are. And I didn't want to think that I wasn't the strong one.

"At least, I didn't want them to know that I wasn't the strong one!

"I never wanted them to see that side of me, when I was needy.

"But I learned that they're there for me. That I could reach out, and ask, and they'd be there for me. They'd insist. They'd be insistent about helping me.

"Again, this was the Hound of Heaven.

"They'd insist on proving to me that I could do it on my own, that I could get out. That I could make enough money to live on. That I could be by myself. *That I didn't have to be by myself.*

"They watched my marriage, and they knew before I did that Tim wasn't going to get another job, that he'd never really be there for me.

"I was almost 64 years old. I wanted someone with me. I wanted someone to live out my life with.

"But he was never really there for me.

"My therapist said to me, 'You think he is going to change. What makes you think that?'

"When I was in group, I'd bring up a problem that would arise, and the group would say, 'Why would Tim act any differently than he's always acted?' And I'd think, 'Come on! He'll change. I'll just be persistent. And he'll come around.'

"I guess I was just so full of denial about the fact that this guy wouldn't come through in some areas, I just couldn't believe it. I'd say to myself, 'Of course, he'll do that. It means the end of the world if he doesn't do it.'

"But you know, it didn't matter to him, that it was the end of *my* world."

# Chapter Eleven:
## Remember The Facts

Beatrice told me that her alcoholic husband was like a chocolate Easter bunny: he looked so good, but when she was really close to him, she saw he was hollow.

\* \* \*

Sandra told me she couldn't wait for her second surgery: it was so good to get out of that house and into the hospital, away from the alcoholic.

\* \* \*

Doris decided to leave, after 35 years of an alcoholic, violent marriage. She felt good about it, until her friends said they were shocked and told her:

"He *can* change, honey. Just give him time."

and

"Look at all the years you were together. You don't need to leave after all those years!"

\* \* \*

*What are the facts?*

Friends, even well-meaning ones, are coming to your situation with advice that often stems from *their own* needs and wants. Change is difficult, even for others who are watching your change. They don't know where you'll wind up: where you might move to; if you'll see them as much; if you might like their husbands; if you'll have the same interests, once you change and your world changes. They're scared, and unconsciously may want you to keep the status quo.

And, if you change, maybe they feel they must look at themselves, too, and their choices.

Also, these friends may be ignorant of alcoholism and the

bizarre behavior of the alcoholic. They may think you've been exaggerating, a little. That you could, if you chose to, "put up with it."

* * *

If you are thinking about leaving, do it or don't do it — because *you* choose to stay or leave. Just remember the facts — and don't let your decision be muddied up by other well-intentioned, but ignorant, folks' input.

Only *you* have to live with the results.

# Chapter Twelve:
# It's *Your* Decision Whether Or Not To Separate — It's Not Your Counselor's Decision

I've been concerned, for the past couple of years, about phone calls I've received from spouses of alcoholics, telling me about the advice they had received from counselors. Here is a typical example:

Juanita did an intervention with her alcoholic husband. She was invited to family week at the treatment center. She was then told that she "had severe abandonment issues of her own," and should separate from her husband. She should have no contact with him except by telephone, and just "work on her issues."

I get calls like this a lot, lately. Calls that come from frightened family members who are regularly told this by counselors:

a) the family member cannot get well in that relationship

or:

b) the alcoholic cannot stay sober in that marriage.

Let's look at these issues:

It is true that most families of alcoholics have severe abandonment fears. However, one does not necessarily have to separate from another person to deal with these issues. Many persons have successfully detached from the effects of someone else's alcoholism and have learned to deal with their abandonment issues through programs such as Al-Anon.

Furthermore, it is not necessarily a virtue to force an issue when one is not yet ready to deal with it — in order to prove that "you are really working on your program of recovery." Isn't the goal "progress rather than perfection"? Who do you need to prove what to? Could this be another manifestation of people-pleasing?

Also, when a counselor tells a visiting family member that their abandonment issues are getting in the way of progress of that family unit, the implicit message to the newly-sober person may be that this fear of abandonment is part of the reason for his alcoholism — instead of the true message: nothing got you drunk. (And, when the counselor goes further and angrily confronts the family for "being enablers" — does this not also imply that "something got him drunk"?)

*　*　*

Could it be that some counselors may be adult children of alcoholics who have not yet resolved their old anger toward their own non-addicted parents? Do they still expect that parent to have: a) been perfect or b) thrown out the alcoholic when the parent couldn't do that?

*　*　*

And what if the couple who've been married 46 years do listen to the counselor who tells them that he can't stay sober around her? Suppose they break up and he still can't stay sober? Is the counselor going to be around to pick up the pieces? I personally feel it's dangerous to give advice to people to break up — or stay together — when it is the client who has to live with the consequences.

I've seen too many counselors "shooting from the hip" and advising couples they've just met on a one-week intensive family unit to dissolve decades-long marriages.

Now, of course there are times when it is probably advisable for a person to *not* return home after completing an inpatient stay for alcoholism (for instance, if the spouse they would be returning to is actively alcoholic or violent). But even in those cases, there are many times when the trauma of separation is too much to deal with, on top of newfound sobriety. Many women, especially, have found it immensely helpful to attend a large number of A.A. *and* Al-Anon meetings every week. When they attend both groups regularly, they are often able to stay sober *and* stay in the marriage long enough to buy themselves *time*. The Al-Anon meetings give them emotional detachment from the marriage problems, so that they *can* stay in that familiar environment, for awhile, at least. Later (and sometimes it takes years), they have the strength to look at leaving a still-drinking and/or violent spouse. If leaving the marriage had been insisted on from the beginning, many of those now-sober women would not be sober, today.

– 37 –

But this is all a *very* individual decision, based on more issues than a single "dysfunctional family" diagnosis. Many women alcoholics find it too frightening, in early sobriety, to deal with facing the world alone and financially-strapped, with young children; many people have never lived alone; many alcoholics — looking to bolster their already-irresponsible attitude toward their families — seek an excuse to further abandon them, instead of becoming responsible, making amends, and seeing if the marriage can be saved.

Now, of course, many relationships and marriages are just not salvageable. But even in those cases, it is often wise to wait a while to make a major change.

The oldtimers in A.A. used to say: No major decisions the first year, if possible. They *knew* that it's often easier for alcoholics to run, rather than to "sit still and hurt." They *knew* that in the first year of sobriety, your brain is so foggy that many of your decisions are probably *way* off base. It's often easier to wait a bit to clear the brain rather than to act impulsively and later try to retrieve a lost partner.

# Chapter Thirteen:
# Perfectionism

"Perfectionist" is often what the alcoholic calls us, when he or she is trying to make us stop talking about alcoholism.

"You're always trying to get the perfect husband! Well, I'm not here on earth to try to live up to your idea of what I should be!" he cries to you, as he continues to drink.

*Is* wanting him to be sober a "perfectionistic" requirement? Do you have the right to demand recovery before you will return to that marriage?

Let's look at this.

Think back to when you were younger. What were your dreams about the perfect husband or wife? Did your list of attributes include "sobriety"?! Did you even consider that a great husband or wife, meant "not passed out"?!

Of course not.

It is not "perfectionism" to have an expectation that your spouse be not-unconscious.

It *is* part of the disease for the alcoholic to call you a "perfectionist" when you expect bottom-line things — like consciousness and breathing — from a marriage.

*       *       *

"Perfectionism" is involved in another issue in our recovery.

We who've lived with alcoholism for a while, are good at *not* telling ourselves the truth about situations or people. We easily ignore and/or defend the alcoholic's serious character flaws, in order to stay in the situation. Because of this deep-seated habit, our uneasiness — our dis-ease — runs very deep.

We have a lot of issues to deal with at most times, so we must decide which issue to deal with, first. However, we often skirt the important issues, and put off and ignore the mountains. We often prefer to deal only with the molehills. But that makes us learn to adapt to a certain low level of un-ease, of dis-ease.

We really do know when we ignore what's important.

But when we are in recovery, we cannot, as much, ignore our issues.

And one of the reasons why we don't want to make a decision is that we fear that perhaps we'll be wrong.

* * *

How can we look at this differently?

We can live with our mistakes!

We can quickly see many options resulting from mistakes — because we don't use time needlessly beating ourselves up, but go right on to looking at alternatives!

Maybe an alternative might have been better for us? Perhaps God has something better in store for us? Maybe we weren't supposed to have the choice we went after?

How do we know, ahead of time, if "we made the *right* choice"?

We won't know.

No one knows, for sure. That doesn't have to stop us from acting, despite our not-knowing. And despite the fact that part of the time, we'll make the wrong choice. *Of course*, you'll have doubts.

Even the saints had doubts.

# Chapter Fourteen:
## Courage To Change The Things We Can

Sometimes, we don't "make a decision" to change a bad situation. Instead, we "hit a bottom" about it and we find ourselves *just changing!*

Susan G. is a financial services counselor. She counsels people from her home-office, often by telephone.

Her alcoholic father lived with her. Sometimes, when she was on the phone with clients, he would have outbursts of temper that could be heard through the house, and clients would ask what it was about. It disturbed the clients and her train of thought, so that she was less able to concentrate on the matters at hand.

Susan got tired of putting up with it. She angrily told her father that he'd have to stop. When she yelled at him, "What do you want me to do — rent an office somewhere so they can't hear you?!" — her father had the arrogance to say "Yes."

After thinking about it for a minute, Susan realized that that put the onus on *her*, when it was *his* problem. She then told her father that if it happened again, he would have to leave the house whenever she had a phone appointment with a client.

\* \* \*

Sandra's son, Ted, was only twelve when he began to confront his father about his drinking, bringing up the subject and talking about the value of Alcoholics Anonymous.

His father then tried to divert and scare him by saying that he'd stop giving him rides to places, saying "I'll not be your taxi anymore."

Ted answered him with: "There are not too many ways you take care of me anymore. One of them is putting food on the table and one is giving me rides, sometimes."

His father said, "Maybe you and I need to see a therapist to iron out our differences."

Ted answered with: "Why don't you just go and see an alcoholism counselor and take the first step towards your own recovery, and then we will talk about counseling together."

Sandra was stunned to see how well her son was. He was not conned into thinking that the problem was one of "communications." He *knew* that it was alcoholism, and that his father could not learn to be straight with his feelings and actions unless he got sober first.

*    *    *

Both of these examples showed courage. What happened to Susan G. and Ted was that they had spent much time in family recovery meetings, and prepared themselves for the time when they would be able to stop putting up with what was unacceptable to *them*.

That is an important point: No one can tell you what is acceptable to *you*. Everybody has some thing(s) that if a person "crosses over that line," are just too offensive to put up with.

In recovery, we get dignity. And that is God-given. It becomes very important because it is a solid and healthy barometer of what can and cannot be done to a child of God.

# Chapter Fifteen:
# "I Was Able To Decide To Leave, Even Though He Was Sober And I Was Physically Ill"

This is Caroline's story:

"We had just gotten married, and we were living in the State of Washington. He was going to get this big job, and all of a sudden, he announced that he lost it. Suddenly, he's out of work, and needs someone to take care of him.

"I kind of knew from his background that he was in and out of work all the time, but I wanted to ignore it. Actually, I had met him years before, when we were still in high school. And he had that reputation back then, as kind of a "slough-off." But he was charming. So, like I said, I ignored it.

"Now, I can look at the picture, and it's so obvious. But, when you're in the middle of it, you don't see it.

"He continued to womanize. He'd been known for it, but I thought that if we got married, he'd be so happy with me, he wouldn't do that anymore.

"And then I had surgery for blood clots. And I had other things wrong with me, physically. I was a mess. And here I was married to an unemployed womanizer. And me trying to work and support both of us.

"I mean, it was on our honeymoon that he started telling me that I've got to get a job.

"He'd get good jobs, but he wouldn't keep them for more than six months. And after he got out of treatment and came home, I saw that he was the same person and he would never change. I just knew it. And I was right. He was the same conniver, the same con man.

"I asked him, when he got out of treatment, 'What did the guys do, when they left the treatment center?' And he answered, 'They went back to work.' And I said, 'What about you?' And he answered, 'What do you want me to do? Go to work for a lousy $15,000 a year?' And I said, 'It beats nothing.' He walked away in a huff.

* * *

"I realized he wasn't going to go back to work. And that I was going to have to support him the rest of my life. Oh, he was going to do little odd jobs and maybe bring in a hundred dollars a month. And he was going to get real excited about it, like a little kid.

"But, it would always have to be a job he liked. He'd never do anything he didn't enjoy doing. *I'd* have to, to support him. But, not *him*."

"He went to a lot of A.A. meetings. And they told him there that he'd have to change. But he didn't want to. And he didn't. Oh, he found socialization; and he found friends; and he found God.

"But, he didn't find a *job!*

* * *

"Well, I wanted out. But, I was scared, because I was so ill.

"But, I was able to leave because the future with him was more devastating than a future alone. If I'd need a person to care for me, medically, I knew *he* wouldn't. Let's put it this way: he said he would. But, I knew better. He'd do it for awhile, and make a big to-do about it. But, he'd get tired of it quick, just like the jobs.

"So, I left. And got an apartment. The first night in this apartment, I couldn't get my window closed. I was weak from the illnesses, and I couldn't close the window. I was frantic! I called a friend who lived up the street, and she came over and closed the window.

"And when I had to get my groceries, I was breathless and exhausted. I found that I had to curtail certain things. I would have to get them into the house, and then sit down for awhile. I would have to learn to do things one step at a time. I'm learning to take care of myself. I'm learning to *not* do certain things. And that's hard for me, because I think I was born running!

"You see, I'm an adult child of an alcoholic, and I think I should be able to do everything! I think there is something amiss if you don't take care of the world!

"Once, I got a maid. And I cleaned for two hours before she came! For two reasons: one, so she'd think well of me, and

- 44 -

another, to lessen her load — because I had to lessen *everyone's* load in life! Except my own.

"We have so little that we need. That we *think* we need. We get a peanut and we give an elephant. We don't ask for a lot. But, if we should happen to get it anyway, we feel so guilty, we give them a thousand times more.

"The point is, after I left, I had to learn all this about *me*. And, it's been quite a wonderful journey."

# Part Three:
## Getting Advice You Can Trust

# Chapter Sixteen:
## Share Your Story With Discretion

Cheryl was doing just fine. Her grandson's Christening was approaching. She had made plans to stay at the ceremony for only as long as the religious rites lasted. She was going to skip the social, planned for afterwards — held at the home of the most abusive members of the family.

She had plane tickets and planned to leave for an island vacation immediately after church that day. *Nothing* was going to spoil her vacation: not the thought of her ex-husband being there with his new drinking-buddy girlfriend; not the thought of her druggie son, who was also the baby's father; not the thought of her daughters who worked for their father, and who sided with him because he bought them off with new cars and high-tech playtoys.

\* \* \*

Cheryl was getting her kitchen redone. She was at the beginning stages, where a designer would come to her house and help her look through catalogs and choose colors, textures, and styles.

Gail, the decorator, showed up early. Together, they went through the books. Cheryl chose lovely florals in blues, mint, and peach. Over coffee, they discussed when the work should start. Cheryl said she'd like to have it done by the middle of April, before she went on vacation.

They schmoozed about vacations in general, and Cheryl told her about the Christening, and how she planned to leave right afterwards.

Gail, who never lived with alcoholism, and who could not possibly comprehend the bizarre abuse Cheryl had been subjected to, answered: "But, how could you? You owe it to your family to be at the reception! You should even be having a reception here for them! After all, it's your grandchild!"

The guilt hit Cheryl like a ton of bricks. She felt as if the six months spent in Al-Anon meetings and counseling had just gone down the drain.

It took many heart-wrenching hours of crisis counseling with Cheryl to help restore the gains she had previously made — so that she could continue with her original self-protective vacation plans.

* * *

We can talk things through; we can have insights; we can finally clearly see the truth about the alcoholism . . . and yet, if we have but a smidgen of self-doubt, even a stranger can erode much of our new-found confidence that we're doing the right thing. (That's because we are so new at it. It gets easier!)

* * *

Meanwhile, it is *so* important for us to discuss what is going on in our lives *only* with other recovering families or counselors who truly understand the craziness of alcoholism.

Well-intentioned persons who have never been subjected to the bizarreness cannot help but say things that are counter-productive because they start from a different framework of reality.

We leave ourselves too open, too vulnerable, when we discuss our stories with just anyone.

Part of our healing derives from acting with self-protection.

We need to *internalize* the fact that we do *not* have to explain ourselves to the world.

# Chapter Seventeen
## "How Counseling Helped Me Decide"

This is Nancy's story of the step-by-step process that helped her to make a decision:

"I was in a group of women from either alcoholic or otherwise-dysfunctional families. The counselor was terrific.

"But, at first, I felt alienated. The others in the group were in their twenties, and I was 49. How could they relate to me? And me to them? I thought they'd never understand my problems. They hadn't been through half of them. They hadn't lived life yet. Their worries were all job concerns, mainly. They hadn't been through marriage, divorce, childbearing, childraising. Well, three out of the ten had. But not most of them.

"They hadn't bought a home, sold a home, lost a home because of an alcoholic. Not yet, anyway. And besides, I had lived with my alcoholic for fifteen years.

"I couldn't share much of myself, at first. I felt intimidated. These girls were young, but sharp! They'd gotten into counseling so young! Actually, I felt a bit jealous that they knew so much and were into getting help so young. They had their whole lives ahead of them, to live healthy.

"One of my difficulties was in confronting my alcoholic husband, Bill. He was an attorney and he ran circles around me. So, my counselor had me practice in the group. She had me tell the members of the group what could be improved about each one of them.

"And that was so hard for me. I am a helper, not a criticizer. I've always felt it was important to be nice to people, even if you might be angry.

"I was never really honest with anyone in the world! I always said what they wanted to hear.

"But what really hurt me was that the group told me that I was so *nice* that they thought I was disgusting! That they didn't trust me!

"Well, driving home from the session, I told them off! In my mind, that is. But two seconds later, I excused them. I told myself that they were raised in rougher neighborhoods than I was raised in, and therefore, they couldn't really help being so brutally frank.

"But, I wrestled with it. I thought about it for days. I told myself that I was basically a nice person, and what's wrong with that? So what if it's a little dishonest?

"But then, I had to admit that I went overboard. That I never said the truth to anyone, hardly.

"There had to be a middle road there, somewhere.

"I had to admit to myself that I was nice and didn't want to hurt people's feelings, which is sweet. But also, I had to admit that I have always been a people-pleaser and afraid of having people mad at me. And that was not necessarily good.

"So, I had to take these two theories, so to speak, and find a middle ground. I told myself that I could no longer people-please so much.

"I had to find a middle ground where I was not brutally honest, but where I was honest with other people.

"That helped me to look *straight* at the things my husband was doing. And that helped me to move closer to making a correct decision, not one based on denial.

\* \* \*

"Then, I began to see where I had things much more in common with the others in the counseling group, than I had previously thought. All of us were trying to learn to deal with things that were to some degree, making us unhappy.

"We were trying to stop repeating the same behaviors. Mine, of course, were all about binding myself so tightly to a man who was going to repeatedly disappoint me, and be unavailable to me, emotionally. He would be nice, and then out of the blue, not nice. I'd been involved with a man before my alcoholic who was like that. He wasn't an alcoholic, but what did that matter? They both were unavailable to me, on any consistent level.

"And of course, my problem was that I continued to adapt to it. Continued to tell myself it would be different. They tell people in A.A. to ask themselves why they do the same things and expect different results. I had to ask myself why I picked the same kind of man and expected him to change — expected different results?

"And why did I continue to deny that I was doing this?

"What helped me so much was, in group, I went over all my life patterns. I looked at all the patterns of my parents and siblings and saw who were my role-models. I said it *out loud*. Before, it was all in my head. But I didn't have a chance to change anything until I said it out loud. It was like, it got out on the table, and therefore I couldn't deny it anymore.

"One of the things I learned about myself — one of my *patterns of behavior* — was that in the beginning of relationships with men, I always believed them, hook, line, and sinker. That is, if they were charming and lovable-seeming.

"I *wanted* to believe them totally. I wanted it to be the way they presented themselves to me.

"I wanted it so badly that I couldn't see it being any other way. Of course, later, after I was so bitterly disappointed in my husband, I told myself the truth about him.

"But what *hooked* me, was my wanting to believe the fairy tales.

"I figured that if I do this, if we do that, all will be okay. And what I was saying to myself, unconsciously, was that if we do this and that, he'll change. He'll be so happy with our relationship, he won't find it necessary to drink or pull away from me.

\* \* \*

"And, then I realized, finally, that I had to leave him. I could not change him. I tried responding differently, but it did no good, in this situation.

"Plus, I had to be honest with myself and admit that I didn't want to adapt to living that way with him, the rest of my life. It made me too depressed.

"It got to the point in my house, that he and I had a silent, unspoken agreement that I was either going to have to give in and accept his behavior for the rest of my life — or leave. It was like we both knew it, once I knew it.

"It's like they really do have radar. They just know when we've had enough."

# Chapter Eighteen:
# What Are Examples Of
# Crazymaking That Counselors
# Should Inherently Know —
# In Order For Us To
# Trust Their Advice-Giving?

I am often asked by families: "How shall I know if my minister understands the craziness I'm living with?" Or: "How will I know if my counselor will be charmed by the alcoholic and think that I am exaggerating the nuttiness? I've been through that scenario once too often!"

* * *

I've devised a list of characteristics of typical crazymaking in the family that helps families when they are looking for a counselor. Family members take this list with them and discuss them with the counselor. If the counselor is not surprised at this list — in other words, if the counselor is familiar with the crazymaking in the alcoholic home — families have told me that they had satisfying relationships with these counselors.

* * *

(This is not at all an exhaustive list, but just indicative of some of the major points of crazymaking in the alcoholic home):

**Some ways alcoholics blame families:**

1) The alcoholic evokes sympathy from you; you feel pity for him; you rescue; he has contempt for you even more.

2) They threaten abandonment over and over, and accuse you of clinging and "having severe abandonment issues."

3) They flirt with everyone you know, and accuse you of being pathologically jealous. *Name of the game: Gaslight* (remember the

old Ingrid Bergman/Charles Boyer film? If not, it might be a good idea to rent it at a video store!)

4) They repeatedly do something outrageously hurtful; you complain and they accuse you of "always accusing them."

**Some universal ways family members tell *themselves* it's *their* fault:**

1) The families take on the blame when the alcoholic is nasty — and give the alcoholic the credit when the alcoholic is nice! Example: Marianne broke up with her alcoholic boyfriend and bemoaned that she would never find another guy "who is such fun." When her counselor met him, he was one step above Sad Sack Joe. Her perplexed counselor asked if he was depressed. "No," they said. He always acted like that! *The truth was: Marianne was the one who injected the fun into their relationship and gave him the credit for it. It never even occurred to her to think that she was the one who kept the relationship alive.*

2) *"Why* am I so upset? He's been nice for two weeks, now." The wife of the alcoholic has lived with his womanizing for thirty-three years, and when he "hasn't done it" for two weeks, she agrees with him that she's "paranoid" when she's afraid he'll do it again. And he's only two weeks sober. *She's taken the junk for thirty-three years and is now taking it in a different form — maybe in a more crazymaking form.*

3) She's been in counseling for six weeks. She tells her counselor that her father, a drinking alcoholic, always beat up her and her mom. She recounts: "When I was ten years old, I started thinking that my mom should not take dad back because mom was getting beaten." What about *her? It didn't even occur to her to want her mom to not take back her dad because he was beating her up, too — and she was the child.*

4) She came home and found him with a drinking-buddy woman in their bed. She "threw a fit" and threw them both out. She got another apartment and moved most of the furniture into it. *When she told her therapist about taking the furniture, she looked nervous and said, "Honest, I deserved it. I worked, too!" How many times do we feel we have to justify our acts of dignity?*

**What are some ways that counselors can misread alcoholic-family signals?**

1) John's alcoholic wife, Augusta, picked up yet another man. She came home and told him that she "didn't want to be married anymore." They went to a marriage counselor who didn't see the alcoholism, and told them: "Augusta seems depressed. Maybe she's just sad and wants to leave you, John." Augusta didn't even remember the counseling session the next day. *Has this counselor ever heard about depression induced by alcoholism?*

2) Melody, recently divorced, was in counseling. Her ex-husband is alcoholic. Three of her four adult children were very anxious to talk with her counselor in a family session. The counselor was pleased with their prompt response to her request to come in for such a session. They, like their father, were charming, quick-witted, alcoholic, and facile in their indictment of their mother. *The facts never emerged about their own drinking and collusion with their father to defend the family's alcoholism. The counselor had no knowledge of the questions to ask to determine whether or not there was active alcoholism in the children. Nor did she even know that this was of prime importance.*

# Part Four:
# Healing After Separation

# Chapter Nineteen:
## "But He Looks So Good Since We're Separated — Maybe He's Not An Alcoholic?"

If the alcoholic "looks good" it doesn't mean he or she isn't alcoholic! "Looking good" is a *stage* of the disease.

\* \* \*

When an alcoholic or other-drug addict reaches a later stage of addiction, he or she needs alcohol or other drugs to *seem normal*. Their bodies are *so* sickened from the toxicity that they need a certain level of drug in them to not go into severe withdrawal.

When they get that level of alcohol or pills into them they seem "calm" and "functional."

But, *they can't stay that way for long*.

For, after they drank or pilled enough to satiate the biochemical need for the drug, the calming — and supposedly "normalizing" — effect begins to wear off.

The withdrawal sets in, and it gives off an anxiety-producing after-effect that lasts longer than did the original anxiety.

As the disease progresses, the calming periods get harder to attain, and the anxiety and/or depressed moods get more difficult to shake.

This cycle continues until sobriety . . . the only way to end the merry-go-round.

\* \* \*

So, don't confuse a seeming "calm" with thinking there's not an addiction. It's just a stage of the disease.

# Chapter Twenty:
## "But He's Drinking Less Since We Separated. Can He Be Getting Better?"

Jan calls me every other week for counseling. She lives in Idaho, and is separated from her husband, Karl. Jan lives in a small town where she can't help but see her husband or hear about him from others. He picks up the kids every other weekend and keeps them until Sunday evening.

Jan has a part-time job as an accountant. She keeps a spotless house and makes all her children's clothing, as well as much of her own. She's a rational woman . . . until he shows up.

Lately, Karl's litany is to keep telling her that he "is controlling his drinking just fine." That he "isn't an alcoholic, like she always thought."

Jan tells me "how well he seems to be doing" and then tells me that he is doing bizarre things in his apartment, like putting dirty ornaments from the yard on the coffee table and thinking they look good. (This is a man who used to be impeccable.)

She insists that he must be better, since he told her so. But, then she adds, in an "oh, by the way" manner: "Oh, he just got out of the hospital. His pancreas is acting up again."

\* \* \*

Denial in the entire family is multi-layered, deep, and subtle. Jan, even though she knew the facts, did not really "hear" when she heard that his pancreas was affected. Jan knew that that was a sign of his progressing alcoholism, but because she lived with Karl's telling her for years that "she was overreactive," she tended to doubt herself. She believed that Karl was really getting better.

\* \* \*

*What is the truth?*

Alcoholism develops in stages: In the first stage, the alcoholic usually has a higher tolerance for alcohol than do other human beings. He or she can drink more and "hold their liquor."

In the next stage, the alcoholic usually can get as toxic from the alcohol as before, *while drinking less of it. It just doesn't take as much booze to get sick.*

Round-the-clock maintenance drinking doesn't usually occur until the last stages of the disease. *So, if your alcoholic husband or wife isn't drinking all the time — and therefore seemingly sometimes "controls" it — it's because he or she has not yet reached that later stage of the disease.*

If you find yourself in denial, note it. Make a "Denial" notebook. Write down your *patterns* in this area. The process of writing them down will enhance your awareness of them when they pop up again. You will be well on your way to recovery when you stay aware of your patterns.

# Chapter Twenty-One:
# "I Can't Stop Being Angry With Him!"

Sandy lives in Michigan. The winters there are not fun for her, especially since she has an illness that lowers her tolerance for cold weather.

Sandy would not be living in Michigan if it weren't for Mike. They married five years ago. She had her own business in real estate in Florida, when she first met her husband.

He was nice for the first three weeks of their marriage. Then, he began the verbal abuse.

Over the years, he had affairs; he drank alcoholically and smoked pot incessantly; and he was off-and-on unemployed. They basically lived on the income from her business.

Sandy started going to a therapist who specialized in families of alcoholics' recovery. She began to change her response to Mike. He got scared and insisted that they move back to Michigan, his home State. He told her he could do better, workwise, but he really wanted to get her away from her therapist.

Scared of losing him, Sandy moved with him.

She had to start all over again, building up a real-estate business, which takes years of work. She got worse, physically, from her illness. She had more bills, therefore, and less income.

And then Mike left.

He is now living off another woman and Sandy will be moving back to Florida when the divorce is final.

But, as she told me, "I want to get on with my life. I partly want to get him back, but mostly, I am so very, very angry. And I feel guilty about it. And I go back and forth between guilt and rage. And I feel stuck."

*   *   *

Sandy's story is typical of women who've been abused and then abandoned. The rage of these women is *not* "inappropriate."

They do not need another person to tell them that "it's time to drop their anger!"

What they need is to know that they certainly have the right to that anger.

But, that *he* does not deserve one more minute of her time!

I wouldn't end the anger for "moral" reasons like "what is *wrong* with you? You are *so* angry and it's been quite a while now?!"

I *would* work on revengefully putting my energy into getting my life back from this horrible person who tried to use and abuse it.

In a short time, you will be miles ahead of the game, while he is hoping that you are still a victim.

And *you* will be *free*.

# Chapter Twenty-Two:
## "When I See My Alcoholic Husband, And He's Nice To Me, I Get Upset!"

Dana hails from Minnesota. She lives there, again, after separating from her alcoholic husband, Ned. Dana moved back to her home State with her two children. She's going through a messy divorce and trying to keep an emotional distance from Ned.

It's even more difficult because when the two of them do have to talk, Ned is usually vicious.

But Dana feels particularly overwhelmed when he is *nice* to her: "When the lawn mower broke, Ned offered to bring me his, when he brought the children back from their weekend with him. It sounds crazy, but *that* got me more upset than anything! Why am I like that? Why shouldn't I be happy when he's nice to me, for a change?!"

\* \* \*

I don't believe there's anything wrong with Dana. I think that she is responding in a very self-protective way, when she doesn't trust his being nice to her.

Why?

a) The "good" stuff can be as manipulative — at least as "hooking" — as the "bad" stuff. Spouses of alcoholics are very often all-or-nothing people. They believe that if it's like it is *now*, it will *always* be.

So, if he's nice now, we think he'll always be.

And where does that kind of thinking lead to? It leads to believing that he's really a wonderful guy, if he lent you that mower.

*We forget the facts of the entire picture.*

*We forget that of course he'll be nice some of the time.*

*No one is not-nice all the time.*

b) When he acts rotten, he's straight-out with it. You don't have to look "over your shoulder" to see the "zinger" that's going to come at you.

So, if he's nice, you naturally become wary. You've been through this one before! Watch out for the next time.

c) You realize that if you are wary, he'll notice it, and point it out, and call you crazy for not being happy that he's being nice to you. "What's the matter with you, *now?*" he yells at you. *He loves to act nice and put you on your guard, so that you'll look overreactive when you're wary.*

d) When you forget the facts, you might partially agree with him that there's something wrong with you because you can't be happy that he's nice to you.

If this happens, remind yourself that this is, once again, the alcoholism rearing its ugly head. *You* are not overreacting.

\* \* \*

*If you're worried that "his friends" may think you're nuts for being wary of a nice-acting man: just think of all the bars in the world with a bunch of alcoholics in there, all complaining (to other drinking alcoholics) about their "paranoid wives."*

*So a motley crew of people whose brains are soaked with alcohol say to each other that you're one of those wives who's "off" for not putting up with their behavior.*

*Think about it.*

# Chapter Twenty-Three:
# "I Can't Forgive Him"

"Toby, what is wrong with me? I can't forgive him! I get so mad at him every time I think about him and this other woman he's living with!"

\* \* \*

I don't personally believe that God is out to get us. I don't believe that He's waiting to zap us for "not forgiving."

Families of alcoholics — we are *so* hard on ourselves. We say, "But it's in the past. Why can't I forgive him?" And we say this when he's *still* doing his junk; when we still see it; when he picks up the children for visitation, and "she" is with him, smirking at us.

This is not "The Past!" This is *now*. And it's incredibly difficult to "forgive" when it's still going on!

Plus — I think that perhaps God wants us to stop tripping over that stone in the road, so that we can get on with our lives, and be useful and productive and effective in helping others. And that can only be completely accomplished by finding peace of mind.

So maybe forgiveness *is detachment*. It may be just a matter of (as Al-Anon so very wisely puts it) "putting our problem in its true perspective" and "not letting it dominate our thoughts and our lives."

\* \* \*

I believe that we get in our own way when we speak of this letting-go process in such a moral way. We are *so* hard on ourselves, morally. We think we not only have to put up with this nonsense, but that we have to put on a saint's face to do it!

It is *so* much harder for us to get some emotional distance from the abuse when we look at our efforts as if *we* must be judged on whether we let go of it well!

What kind of God is that who would see us being abused, and

then punish us for not getting out of it *gracefully?!* Certainly not the God of Mercy and Goodness.

I think when we live with alcoholism for any amount of time, we unconsciously attribute the hostility and anger of the alcoholic (and of our own natural feelings) to our concept of God. Without even knowing it.

\* \* \*

I think He just wants us to learn to be as gentle and nonjudgmental toward ourselves as He really is towards us.

I believe He feels a lot of compassion for us who've lived with the abuse of alcoholism. I think He greatly understands that we often cannot yet come out from under the fear of more abuse — whether we fear that the abuse would come from the alcoholic or from our own alcoholic-family-sickened concept of God.

# Chapter Twenty-Four:
## "My Denial, My Compassion, And My Guilt Pulled Me Down Into It With Him, Again"

Most families of alcoholics go through certain stages of mood swings, after a separation.

They are:

a) Going back and forth between terror and relief and amazement that they had the courage to do it

b) Gratitude to God for helping them

c) Inability to sleep and other signals of situational — temporary — depression

d) Childlike wonder at the vastness of options open, now

\* \* \*

What are other feelings that can lead into setbacks?

If we get into:

☐ Smugness about having the strength to do it

☐ Understandable, continual anger

Anger and self-righteous feelings can carry us through a certain period of time, but they do eventually end. Unfortunately, there is a boomerang effect from extended anger and self-righteousness. Families of alcoholics have much more of a sense of conscience and of "doing what's right" than do other folk. Therefore, we tend to have guilt after we've angered onto someone for a period of time . . . a feeling of "we've got to make it up to them."
This guilt is often subconscious.

What we (unconsciously) tell ourselves is that we need to "make up for our anger" by letting the other person off the hook.

And we do that by going back into denial about how bad their behavior really was.

But, when we tell ourselves, especially unconsciously, that they were not so bad — then, *we* get blamed, because we left them! After all, if they were really just a little annoying, instead of abusive, then why in the world did we make such a big deal out of it, and leave?

We get back into the old behavior of taking the blame. Once again, we collude with the alcoholic in saying: "the family is at fault."

The best way to counteract that is to *write down the facts. Keep a fact-notebook.* That is one of the best ways to end the minimizing that is often at the heart of family denial.

Example of how writing down the facts can help tremendously: Joanne told me about an incident that was so horrible that she ordinarily would have gone into her denial, and forgotten it. But, she had written it down in her fact-file, and could refer back to it when she told herself that he "probably wasn't that bad."

This is what she wrote about:

Joanne and her actively-alcoholic husband, Kirk, were in a marriage-counseling session. The therapist asked Joanne what she would really like from the marriage. Joanne answered that she would like it if Kirk came home at night, didn't drink, that he would be nice, and that he would spend one whole week being good to her.

The therapist asked Kirk if he would spend one entire week being good to her. He shrugged his shoulders and shook his head No. The therapist was stunned that he wouldn't agree to just that.

What I told Joanne that I found incredible is that the marriage counselor didn't ask her a very important question: "Do you mean that in your entire 24-year marriage, Kirk has never been nice to you for seven consecutive days?"

\* \* \*

*Write down the facts. Keep them in a very safe place, so that they cannot be found to later hurt you.*

*We families of alcoholics go so very easily into denial and minimization, that we cannot trust our memories to come up with the truth. (I can't count all the times that clients of mine have remembered something, and exclaimed, "I forgot that that happened!" And it was something like "he shot off guns in the house through the ceiling, all the time!" And the client told me this after weeks of her telling me that he "wasn't that violent.")*

*We must be able to remember the truths when we start to "romance the past." For if we do not, we may have to repeat the past.*

\* \* \*

Another trap we can get into when our anger dies down is: *great compassion for the alcoholic.*

We often think that compassion will keep us at a detached distance from the alcoholic — and then we start thinking we are a step above holy! After all, he's terrible and we're kind and distanced and that leads *easily* into thinking we are *wonderful.*

In reality, that "compassion" is easily done away with as soon as the alcoholic acts up, again. Our feelings then turn into confusion and rage.

\* \* \*

*True detachment doesn't feel noble. Nobility feelings are too transient. To keep it up, you've got to be so good all the time! (Besides, we tend to turn things around and convince ourselves that our family symptoms of sickness are virtues: we say, "I was so good to him. He'll never find another one like me!" Then we go about trying to get a relationship with someone who will appreciate our overly-givingness! When, in reality, that is not a virtue! In fact, if we keep it up, we will just hook into another sickie, because only those kind will "appreciate" our sickness of giving too much. A well person will give a wide berth to someone who has to love too much.)*

\* \* \*

Our fears are the source of our over-abundant need to feel noble. We feel like we've got to be wonderful in order to have God's permission to leave abuse.

That's just not so. We *can* be allowed to leave abuse, even if we aren't "wonderful"; and we can leave even if that abuse does not occur all the time.

The alcoholic doesn't have to be Hitler, in order for us to have permission to leave.


**If your therapist, your friends (maybe even your alcoholic too) are all telling you that you're crazy for continuing to take abuse, then sometimes the one thing that helps is to tell yourself that you're too sick right now to make decisions. So what you'll do is**

go through the motions. Let the lawyer (if he or she is a good one) make the decisions (like "go for half the property" when you want to give it all away to the alcoholic because you feel guilty for leaving). It's sort of like, "Let Go And Let Lawyer."

# Chapter Twenty-Five:
# "I've Dropped The Proceedings
# Six Times, Now"

"I had a protection order against him. He had tried to run me over in a car. He was very drunk. At least, it seemed as if he tried to run me over.

"My counselor told me to look at it for what it was. That he *did* try to run me over. I was actually knocked over a little bit. It would have been much worse, had I not jumped when I saw the car coming at me.

"But I don't want to believe it."

\* \* \*

Sally told me this in her living room. She said her counselor also told her that if she tried to diminish it or minimize it, it was likely to happen again.

\* \* \*

· If we try to diminish the truth of the impact of an event, or if we say it was really not going on, then the next logical step is we don't do anything about it. Then, the alcoholic figures he can get away with it.

\* \* \*

Sally went on: "I had left him before that, for a few weeks, because of his drinking and his leaving me alone all the time.

"I took him back because he promised he'd change.

"Ten days later, he tried to run me over.

"We've been in divorce proceedings six times, now.

"I had to serve him papers each time again, because I always dropped the proceedings.

"Each time, he promised things would get better. And he desperately wanted to believe it, too.

"Things would get better, for a very short while.

"The last three times, he went to treatment to get me back. And then, he'd gradually let up on his A.A. meetings, and drop out and get drunk.

"When I'd say things to him like, 'I have to see the change in you first, before I come back,' he'd tell me I didn't trust him. And I'd feel guilty for not trusting him. So, I'd go back. And he'd get drunk. And then, I'd say, 'See? You got drunk, like I said. I came back too soon.' And he'd come back with, 'It's your fault. You're always on my back. Looking at me. Watching to see if I'll get drunk. Anyone would get drunk with someone always expecting it.'

"Actually, the last time, he didn't promise he'd stop drinking. I guess he know he couldn't — and I wouldn't believe him. So, he promised he'd just drink at home. And I accepted it because I was so lonely for him to be home. At least I'd have a husband at home. And he thought he could control his drinking more at home, then, too. He thought he could be a good father and a good husband, but still be able to drink.

"He does not think he's powerless over alcohol.

"He says he 'just drinks beer.' He thinks that means he's not alcoholic."

* * *

*What to remember, so that you can get out from under the craziness:*

☐ *Alcoholics will blame the family, as surely as tubercular patients will cough.*

☐ *The alcoholic will turn the facts around 180 degrees to accomplish the blame.*

☐ *You do not have to convince them that they're wrong. They know it.*

☐ *When you spend time trying to convince them of the truth, they know that you feel vulnerable. When you do not spend time trying to convince them of the truth, but just go about your business knowing the truth and acting upon it, they know that you know the truth. And they lose their power over you.*

☐ *Making your life plans according to the threats/promises of a person whose brain is soaked with alcohol, is akin to making your life plans according to the wishes of a mental patient.*

☐ *You absolutely have the right to stay away long enough from a relationship in order to see how it will develop and to see if promises will be kept.*

☐ *If a relationship is meant to be, it will happen in good time, and according to God's time.*

☐ *It almost never feels right to do the right thing, for alcoholic families. It almost always makes us feel guilty, at first.*

☐ *If it's good for the family, it's good for the alcoholic.*

# Chapter Twenty-Six:
## "I Feel Guilty Because I Think I Didn't Do Enough To Make Him Want To Be Sober"

Families often say, "I should have recognized his alcoholism. After all, he was an alcoholic when I married him 30 years ago." Well, Baloney! Thirty years ago, who in the world recognized alcoholism? We knew people were drunks, but we didn't know they were alcoholics.

\* \* \*

Anyone who calls you "an enabler" has no concept of what real recovery is. It is important to look at this word and see what it means. Basically, it means that you have cleaned up after the alcoholic's messes: that you have not been able to stop yourself from rescuing him or her from the consequences of their behavior. The reason you rescued the alcoholic is that you either were very fearful for them, or you were afraid of losing the alcoholic's love, or you thought that the alcoholic would leave you if you "stopped putting up with it."

Nobody has the right to fault you: it's blaming the victim. That's a terrible thing to do to the family.

Furthermore, when you call someone an enabler, you are giving the alcoholic yet another excuse for his behavior. I've heard a lot of alcoholics say, "I wouldn't have drunk as long if I hadn't been enabled."

Alcoholism counselors consider it important for recovery when alcoholics stop blaming other people for their drinking. When an alcoholic says that he or she drank because they "were enabled" — they are adding yet another excuse to the repertoire. And that kind of excuse-making kills alcoholics.

That kind of blaming makes it easier for them to go back out and drink — the next time they think they've "been done wrong."

What if you did enable — rescue — this alcoholic? If you did, you were acting from a very normal instinct to love and protect.

Let me quote from an article in the Baltimore *Sunpapers* a few years ago. A reporter was at a local outpatient treatment center where families were gathered to view a film. As they watched, many of the family members became visibly angry. The reporter asked why they were upset, and was told by viewers that in the film they were called "enablers." One woman very articulately stated, "If we love them, we're enablers. If we're angry, we're bitches. When do we win?"

* * *

We've got to stop calling family members "enablers" because they loved.

**Families will stop rescuing when they feel safe enough to do so, when they have lost their fears of losing the alcoholic. Attacking them for "enabling" only increases their fears and feelings of unworthiness.**

We've also got to stop blaming families for being angry when they are naturally angry because of all the junk that's happened. We've got to help families to learn to stop blaming themselves and how to say, instead, "I did my best, I did what I could, I probably did more than anyone else could've done. I've certainly put up with more than my alcoholic would have done, had I acted that way toward him.

"Now, I've got to start believing my recovery is dependent upon my becoming self-centered in a healthy way."

Let's stop putting families in a no-win.

# Chapter Twenty-Seven:
# "I Left A Sober Alcoholic"

Rita's story:

"I left him three years after he had stopped drinking. Nothing had changed. He acted the same and indicated to me that he did not intend to change. I went to two or three Al-Anon meetings a week. The women who were secretaries at these meetings were pretty nonjudgmental about separations and divorce. They stuck to the principles of the program and didn't have opinions they foisted on others.

"I began to face the fact that I had good reasons to leave my marriage. I felt like I had gotten permission from my God, through listening to and watching other women who were separated and who stayed in Al-Anon and helped others to go through what they had to go through. And they grew so much! That's when it finally sunk in to me that I could possibly leave him. I'm not even sure that it was a conscious thought, then.

"Those women were the first women I had met who, when they were divorcing, weren't beating their feet and gnashing their teeth.

"They had their times, of course. And their crying. And their fears. But they were growing through it all. And praying. And looking at themselves. And trying to turn it into a positive experience. A growth time. And they were succeeding — even when they were hurting.

"I think that's the first time that I thought about the fact that it was all right. It was permission from the group and from my God, speaking through those people.

"Those women were leaving their husbands and no one thought the worst of them for it.

"I needed that permission."

\* \* \*

When you meet people in recovery meetings — people you

respect — who leave their abusive spouses, something happens that often gives others "permission" to leave.

Families of alcoholics are so caught up with irrational guilt, they feel they can't leave when the spouse is rotten only part of the time.

A spouse of an alcoholic may believe that God will punish her if she leaves; but she can meet and see other recovering families who are thriving and living and joyous and free — and not being punished, just because they left abuse.

# Chapter Twenty-Eight:
## "If I Give Up Obsession, Do I Have To Give Up Hope?"

Carrie told me that she could not stop spying on her alcoholic boyfriend. And when she wasn't doing that, she was worrying about him or calling him.

Her thinking was: If I give up the obsession, I'm giving up on the relationship.

\* \* \*

I often hear from people how they have a great reluctance to stop obsessing about the alcoholic even long after the divorce is over.

They think that if they give up the obsession, it means they don't care.

If the relationship is meant to be, it *will* happen. But it depresses us when we think that it might not be meant to be, and therefore it wouldn't work out, if we left it up to God. We *want* to believe that if we want something badly enough we can get it.

Why do we want something so much that maybe isn't good for us?

We romanticize. We love the all-or-nothing about everything. We get bored when things are peaceful. If there isn't "stuff" going on, we "stir things up."

It can be very helpful if people look at what's going on in their lives when they start obsessing again.

Are you bored? Do you want some excitement after that week at work? Do you have pre-menstrual syndrome? Is there a full moon? Is there a change in the seasons? Is holiday time arriving? Are you trying to escape from painful memories, or from facing your future?

It is good to know what's going on. Then, we can stop giving so much power to the person we're obsessing about. If we stay unaware, we tend to say "Oh, I must be thinking about him because he is So Wonderful or the attraction must be so over-whelming."

In reality, it could be nothing more than the fact that you've just gotten over the flu and are therefore temporarily more vulnerable to obsession.

Also, it's important to remind ourselves that we tend to lump everything together. We say, "If I give up the obsession, I give up hope." Perhaps you are really saying, "I enjoy the highs and hate the lows, but I'm willing to pay and go through the lows because I want the highs."

But if you're obsessive because he continually leaves and you can't stop thinking about him, then there's a good chance nothing will change if somebody doesn't break the patterns.

\* \* \*

There is hope for recovery, but that is different from obsessively worrying.

Recovery includes being willing to go through the grief of giving up the excitement of the obsession.

A.A. people talk about "Romancing the past" — talking about the excitement, the fun, as if it were still fun.

The A.A. oldtimers talk about getting realistic and stop living in the past. When you think about it, obsessing about what's over is like "spending your time with an empty chair." That's not a person.

One of our problems, when we come from alcoholic families, is we can very easily slip into pretending that what is not real, is real. And letting that emptiness be enough for us.

\* \* \*

This is all very difficult to deal with. But, as a wise friend once told me, "You've got to want to get well more than you want anything." And when you reach that point, that's when you're at the turning point of recovery, and you really get well.

If you haven't yet reached that point, it's okay. Much of getting well is self-acceptance. Accepting yourself *where you are*. So if you haven't reached that point where you *really* want to face reality, where you *really* want to give up the excitement of obsession, you must tell yourself that *that's* okay.

Be reassured that further along your particular recovery path, you will be moved to a different, more enjoyable place. And that does not necessarily mean that you will not be with that person in a happy relationship! It just might be that you will be more able to deal with him or her differently: with you being much less vulnerable, feeling safer, and not at his or her mercy any longer.

*   *   *

Just be willing to give up the *edges of your pain*. That's when you start becoming willing to change. It doesn't usually happen all at once. It's a process. And, if you start very slowly, that's quite enough.

# Chapter Twenty-Nine:
## "How Can I Help Him After We're Separated?"

Mary E. asked me this:

"My husband is an alcoholic. We are separated. I told him I cannot live that way. I don't, however, want to get divorced. I want him to get help. There is no way to get his job to do an intervention. They all drink with him, including his boss.

"I do have some influence; he still loves me. He's just not ready, yet. I'm going about my life, and I'm not focusing on him. But I want to give it some time before I'm ready to take further steps to finalize the separation. To see if maybe he'll get some help on his own.

"My question is: What can I say to him when he calls me in a drunken rage? I don't want to make the situation worse. But, I don't want to take the abuse, either."

\* \* \*

I told Mary, "Say this to him only once: 'John, I love you and know that this rage is caused not by you, but by your disease. It makes you want to get so angry that you have an excuse to go get drunk. It wants to kill you. And I want you to live. I'm going to hang up the phone and not listen to your disease giving me this abuse. Good-bye for now.' "

Mary wrote this down and kept it near her phone, so that when he called, she could say this and not count on having to remember it when she was so upset.

It was one of the things that John later said helped drive a wedge between him and his alcoholism.

What was equally important was, that phone call allowed her to express her self-protection and her dignity and yet left no residual guilt!

She hoped it helped him, too; but she knew that she was only in charge of efforts — not results. She prayed and put it in God's hands. That let her be free and not waste her life in ineffectual efforts to make his life different.

It's not a moral issue, this letting-go business. If controlling things *worked*, we'd all be pretty successful! Instead, what *does* work is to let go of results!

# Chapter Thirty:
# What Are The Real Problems
# About Dating Again?

Karen called me from San Jose. She wanted to talk on the phone and have co-dependency counseling after breaking up a ten-year marriage.

Karen said she thought the problem in her marriage was that she "had wanted to marry a dentist." Her mother had married a dentist; her grandmother had married a physician; and "the expectation was there."

Karen did *not* marry a dentist, however, as I learned when we talked further over the weekend. She married a *dental school dropout* who laid claim to *being* a dentist. He merely insinuated to the world that he was working on it to become one, and wasn't Karen lucky that she found him!

Fact: Karen and he were both 35 years old, and it had been 10 years since this man had set foot in a dental school!

Karen's main problem was not (as she thought) that she "wanted to live through his success." *The bottom line problem with alcoholic family members goes deeper. Other women try to find themselves through their men, and see later that they have to "fill the hole in the soul" in perhaps other ways. But when we come from the craziness of living with alcoholism, we believe lies. We go after the doctor-marriage and marry instead the unemployed actor and tell ourselves "he'll be a doctor, yet." And he is 50 years old!*

Most people who marry alcoholics or other-drug addicts have certain things very much in common.

We think that "denial" means only that we say to ourselves (or believe them when they say it) that the drinking/other-drugging is less than it is.

*Denial is also when we tell ourselves that what is, isn't; and when we tell ourselves that we really don't see what we do see.*

\* \* \*

*Solution:*

a) *Pay attention to cues.* We who are used to living with alcoholics, are past-masters at saying to ourselves that the cues are not there. They are. Write down all that was said and done if you start dating, and bounce it off someone who understands alcoholic-family patterns.

b) *Don't minimize.* We believe, by now, that we "overreact" or that we "make too much out of stuff." *We do not. We do the opposite. We make mountains into molehills.*

c) *Trust your gut.* If you have lived with alcoholism, and you get that same gut-wrenching feeling from this new guy . . . be careful!

d) *Remember that we tend to totally overlook the one or two facts that bluntly point out that we are correct when we assess a situation.*

   Case in point: a client of mine told me how his alcoholic wife and addicted children all thought he was crazy when he claimed they were addicts. Their "proof" of it was: he admitted his brother into a treatment center. The wife and kids said the brother had no business being there because "he was not an alcoholic."

   I asked this man to talk about his brother. About two hours later, he mentioned that the brother's next-door neighbors asked him (my client) to "do something about his brother's trash." When he inquired what they meant, they told him they were appalled at all the empty booze bottles each week.

   Now, this vignette was disclosed to me as a "by the way." *It was not seen by my client as significant. And yet, it was the "proof" he needed to validate that his brother was indeed an alcoholic.* We believe the lies because we think we cannot possibly be right, and "they" must always be right.

\* \* \*

Should you date again? Can you trust yourself to pick a healthy person? I think we don't get well in a vacuum. You may not be ready today, to date. But part of the "reason" given for not venturing out is "I'm not ready!" *Oftentimes "not ready" means not ready for marriage. Being from alcoholic families, we are "all or nothing!" "Dating" doesn't mean get married today. It means have dinner!*

Slowly, we can learn to evaluate people; not minimize; not say we are crazy when we know we are not. And when we have mastered this pretty much, we are not at all as much at risk, like we were before, to marry the first alcoholic or emotionally-unavailable person who comes along.

# Part Five:
## Special Issues

# Chapter Thirty-One:
# Answering Your Legal Questions About Alcoholism, Divorce, Children, and Court-Ordered Evaluations

An Interview With David G. Evans, Esq.,
Chair of the Alcoholism and Drug Law
Reform Committee, of the Individual Rights
and Responsibilities Section of the
American Bar Association

Mr. Evans has a law practice in Lawrenceville, New Jersey, concentrating on substance-abuse issues including family law, drug testing, and employment law. In 1985, he was invited to the White House by President and Mrs. Reagan in honor of his work on youth, alcohol and drug problems for the American Bar Association. Evans is also the author of three books: *A Practitioner's Guide to Alcoholism and The Law; Kids, Drugs, and the Law;* and *Drug Testing Law, Technology, and Practice.*

**DREWS: When you have custody in a divorce, how do you protect your children if the alcoholic picks them up for the weekend, and is driving drunk?**

EVANS: If the person is drunk when picking the child up, I would call the police. Let them come out and document that the person is intoxicated and may be driving a car. If the drinking parent leaves before the police show up, at least you have a record that you did call the police. You tried to get an objective party, i.e., the police, to review the matter. And if the non-custodial parent leaves before the police get there, you can use that to show the person was intoxicated. Of course, you should contact your attorney. The best course of action is to discuss this with your attorney before it happens, and let your attorney advise you on what you should do.

**DREWS: Suppose the alcoholic says, "I left because my -ex was acting crazy again; accusing me of stuff. I just didn't want to go through all this. I wasn't drunk. She was trying to prejudice the children against me and she was trying to not let me have the kids."**

**EVANS:** The response to that can be: "Well, look, next time when you come to the house to pick up the child and you're intoxicated, I'll call the police again. And if you want to prove you're not intoxicated, then just stay there. Let the police officer check you out!"

I would then, as much as possible, document what had occurred. And, if you can, when the alcoholic non-custodial parent shows up, have somebody there to witness it — somebody who will be seen as being credible by the court.

**DREWS: It might only be a neighbor.**

**EVANS:** It could be a neighbor. There is no reason that a neighbor would have an axe to grind. It should be an objective party. You could even hire an investigator. But basically, if you can, just get someone to be able to certify that the non-custodial parent showed up intoxicated — this would back you up. It could even be two or three witnesses — that would be fine.

Additionally, you could call the police and say, "Look, this guy was just here. He's driving a blue Ford. This is his car's license number. Go pick him up." If he gets arrested for drunk driving, you have made your case.

In New Jersey, the courts are pretty good. If one of the parties alleges that the other party is an alcoholic, there most likely will be an investigation. And they're pretty thorough.

We have [in New Jersey] what they call a "Juvenile Family Crisis Law." If a parent or guardian of a child is not taking proper care of that child (and it doesn't have to be abuse or neglect; it could be alcoholism) — the child, or anyone concerned about the child, can file a complaint with the Court, and under the law, the parental alcoholism must be investigated. If they are found to be alcoholic, they may be sent to treatment. The law mandates — *mandates* that the alcoholic parent be investigated.

Also in New Jersey, under the domestic-violence law, if somebody is found guilty of domestic violence — and it doesn't have to be a criminal complaint — the victim can get a court order that orders treatment for the abuser. If the victim is a child, anybody who has an interest in the child can file one of those complaints.

Anyone who is a victim can just go down to the police station and file a complaint, and ask that the person receive treatment.

Delaware has an excellent Family Court Act. There doesn't even have to be a divorce! If a family member files a complaint saying the person is an alcoholic — the term that's used is that "they are imperiling a family relationship" — the Court could order the whole family into treatment.

\* \* \*

**DREWS: How can families find out what laws are available for them to use in their State?**

EVANS: There are a couple of sources of information. One is, you can go to your County prosecutor's office and ask there. They will help you with domestic violence laws.

I would see if you have a family court in your State. I would inquire there for information. But, not all States have family courts. So, you could then go to a law library. Every State has a State law library and you can ask the law librarian for information, and they'll refer you to statutes for you to read. All law schools have libraries, and your County courthouse may also have one.

**DREWS: You don't have to be a lawyer to go to the law library?**

EVANS: No. You can go to the law library and say, "I'm looking for all the laws that have to do with such-and-such," and they'll help you find it.

You can also talk to some matrimonial attorneys and they'll have some information. You can also go to your State child-protective agency. (That goes by a different name in every State.)

**DREWS: You just call the telephone information operator and ask for the number for general information for your State government offices? And when you reach them, tell them what you're looking for and they can direct you to the right number?**

EVANS: Right! And there may be similar offices on a County level. Maybe a County child protective agency, a County public defender, a County prosecutor. There also may be a domestic violence program. County domestic violence programs are also a very good source to find out things.

\* \* \*

**DREWS: How do you get a court-ordered evaluation that is effective?**

**EVANS:** In court, you should start asking for a professional, objective evaluation as early as you can in the case. You can make sure that the evaluation will be done properly.

**DREWS: How do you make sure it will be done properly?**

**EVANS:** You ask that it be done according to specific criteria. Here are four examples:

a) Ask that the MAST test be used: that's the Michigan Alcohol Screening Test.

b) There is also the DSM III-R test. That's the Diagnostic Statistical Manual III-R of the American Psychiatric Association. They have evaluation criteria in there for substance abuse.

c) You can also use the Mortimer Filkins Test.

d) And there's the McAndrews Scale on the Minnesota Multiphasic Personality Test (M.M.P.I.).

**DREWS: How do families make sure these tests are used?**

**EVANS:** When you go to court, have your lawyer ask for all four tests to be given — or at least one or two. If you can help it, you don't want the court to send the person for evaluation to a psychiatrist or psychologist who doesn't understand that alcoholism is a primary disease.

**DREWS: Now suppose the court has a pattern of sending people for evaluations to a certain psychologist who believes alcoholism is a mental health problem and not a primary disease. Suppose this psychologist administers any of these four tests. Is he or she going to interpret it correctly?**

**EVANS:** They can, yes. Ask that it be done according to those criteria.

**DREWS: In other words, if you don't ask for at least one of those four tests to be used, the evaluator may just use his or her own questionnaire. And that is often ineffective in diagnosing alcoholism. At least, do you have a better chance at a correct evaluation if one or more of these four tests is used — even if the evaluator isn't the best?**

**EVANS:** Yes! Also, most States have a statutory definition of alcoholism. That means that somewhere in the State laws, there is a law that defines alcoholism. And the majority of the States have a definition.

**DREWS: What good does that do?**

**EVANS:** Again, it's an objective evaluation, a legal evaluation.

Have that standard applied to the person's drinking.

**DREWS: If you have a terrible evaluator, is there any way to get a second or third opinion?**

EVANS: You certainly can. Usually the courts will not prohibit you from getting another opinion, but it's going to depend on the situation. I can't say that in all cases the court is going to allow that.

**DREWS: How do you find out who are the evaluators for the court and whether or not they are good? And how would you go about lining up evaluators for an initial or second opinion (should you need it) that the court would accept?**

EVANS: You can make a due-process argument: The law says that a person can't be deprived of a right, or property or freedom, without due process of the law. The law has to have a reason for what it's doing — has to do it according to a fair method.

So, when you go in to ask for an evaluation, you can say, "We think the evaluation ought to be done according to professional standards." Using the DSM III is difficult to challenge because it is the American Psychiatric Association's evaluation standard — and very highly regarded.

You should submit those criteria to the court, and say, "Look, we're talking here about being fair. We're talking here about using professional, objective criteria. These are the criteria that are recognized nationally and internationally. And we think the evaluation should be done according to these criteria, and that the court should appoint someone to do the evaluation *who is trained in these techniques.*"

**DREWS: If you gather a list together (to present to the court) of names of good evaluators — does a person have the right to say to the court, "We have these evaluators' names that could be used. These are people in the community who are known for being able to give professional evaluations around these issues"? Will the court take these suggestions?**

EVANS: They may or may not. The court may look at that and say, "Well, you're just going to give me counselors that are weighted toward your side." But, then, you can say to the court, "We will welcome the defendant also submitting a list of counselors who use these techniques. And we'll see if we can agree on one." That's how it's done in arbitration.

**DREWS: Can a spouse of an alcoholic go to court and say, "I don't want a divorce — I want a legal separation. And I would like to**

have you evaluate him and make him go to treatment (if you find alcoholism)"?

EVANS: You certainly can do that, but again, it's going to be dependent on State law and the attitude of that particular court. You can do that in New Jersey, you can do it in Delaware, you can do it in a number of other States. Again, do what I recommended earlier: go to the sources I talked about to find out what your particular State laws are.

\* \* \*

DREWS: How do you find an attorney who understands alcoholism? (And here's why most people are concerned with this: If they retained an attorney who didn't understand alcoholism, the lawyer often felt their client was exaggerating when they were describing what it was like, living with an alcoholic. That it couldn't be *that* crazy. All that, added to the crazymaking the family was already going through.) That's why families ask, "How can I find somebody who at least understands what's going on?"

EVANS: Let me start off by saying that, if somebody is just committed to getting a divorce, you are in far better shape by just getting a good divorce lawyer. A divorce is usually settled on financial issues. If there are children, of course, custody becomes an issue. Then you need somebody who really knows divorce law.

DREWS: Your suggestion, then, is to get a wonderful divorce attorney. That's Number One.

EVANS: Right! I've had clients that wanted to use the divorce to prove that the husband was an alcoholic. They are really losing sight of the fact that most divorce cases don't even go to trial. So there is never going to be any "proving" or not that he is an alcoholic. Usually, most divorce cases resolve around financial settlements, and child-custody issues, if there are any children.

DREWS: But, around child-custody issues, parents are saying to me, "I want to prove that he is an alcoholic, because I don't want him having custody. Not only do I not want him to have custody, but I don't want him to be able to pick the kids up when he's drinking."

EVANS: If the attorney is not knowledgeable about alcoholism, I would try to educate the attorney. I would have the attorney talk to a counselor; give him or her something to look at or read, about the subject.

Also, even if the court believes that a parent is an alcoholic, it doesn't necessarily mean that they are going to deny visitation to the alcoholic.

**DREWS: What most people are talking about is not denying visitation. What most people are talking about is wanting restrictive driving. As parents have said to me, "I'm willing to have my kids see their father. But I want the kids picked up in a taxi because he's always drunk!"**

EVANS: That's just going to be a matter of doing the documentation and proving to the court. And it's also dependent on the attitude of the court and the attitude of the State.

About providing the proof: there's no magic around that. It's knowing what are the symptoms of alcoholism, and documenting it in the parent.

Also, perhaps the judge can talk to the children about it and ask, "Does your dad drink when he drives with you?" And of course, the more the attorney knows about alcoholism, the more he's going to be able to take the signs and symbols of alcoholism and translate them into court documents.

**DREWS: One problem about the kids. Even when the kids see their father drink, a lot of them are scared that they may lose their father's love if they "tell on him." That's how kids see it. How do you handle that in your office when you have a five-year-old who says, "Yes, my Daddy does pick me up when he's drinking!"**

EVANS: I think the whole family really needs pre-divorce counseling. About what to expect and how to go through it. The kids need to be educated about alcoholism even before the divorce is initiated, if possible. Kids need to be made aware and get into counseling as soon as possible. It's all part of the process.

* * *

**DREWS: Is there a way to court-order an intervention? Can you do it without the court telling the alcoholic that you had anything to do with it?**

EVANS: In some States like New Jersey and Delaware, upon receiving a complaint, the court can get everybody together and say, "What's going on here? We're going to investigate this." And if they can find that the alcoholic needs treatment, they can send him to treatment. But you can't do it anonymously. You can't call up the court and say, "I want you to do something about my husband, but don't say I'm involved." You have to come forward.

**DREWS: Can you get this intervention done in most States?**

EVANS: In many States, in any number of ways, yes. In some States they have commitment laws for alcoholism. I believe Minnesota is an example, where you can file a complaint, have it investigated, and have a commitment to treatment. Some places, it's easy to at least get an evaluation. In other States, it's difficult because the criteria are so hard to meet to get somebody committed to treatment. They'd have be a chronic, totally out-of-control alcoholic. Like the skid-row type. In most States, it's not easy, but it's not horribly difficult to get somebody committed for treatment.

It's not often done, because people are not aware they can do it. We had a law like that in New Jersey for years that nobody ever used.

**DREWS: How do people find out about this in their State?**

EVANS: Again, I would go to the law library; I would go to the family attorney; I would go to the prosecutor's office.

But you can also use an attorney as a threat, to force an intervention. Say a wife wants an intervention. Her attorney can write a letter to the husband, stating that the lawyer has been retained to resolve the family problem caused by the husband's alcoholism. The attorney can outline the wife's rights.

The attorney may also be able to attend an intervention, as long as it's okay with the laws and ethics rules.

**DREWS: You can do this to add to your clout for an intervention!**

EVANS: That's exactly right. Or the wife can say, "I've consulted with an attorney." I've had people come to me to talk to me and set this up. And we've used this clout to force treatment, and there didn't have to be a divorce, after all. Because he went to treatment.

I would use the law *and* I would get counseling, because there are a lot of issues. I think people come in thinking that the law can resolve their emotional issues, and it can't. They need counseling to do that.

**DREWS: I suggest that if they're going to get divorced, or separated — when they go through this process, have a counselor holding your left hand and a lawyer holding your right hand. While your body is sitting in an Al-Anon meeting!**

**EVANS:** That's right! It helps everybody. It helps the lawyer, too, because the situation can get very bad. You need to plan this out. Recognize that it's a serious commitment, what you're undertaking.

*   *   *

**DREWS: What recourse do spouses of alcoholics have, worldwide?**

**EVANS:** I would say that, as primitive as things are here, the United States is way ahead of the rest of the world. There are some countries that have good programs in effect. For example, in Sweden, if you have an alcoholic husband who didn't pay child support, the court of the Swedish government will pay the child support for you. And then they will go after the husband. But, generally, in Europe, their attitude about alcoholism is about 20 or 30 years behind ours.

**DREWS: It would be hard to get any kind of evaluation done in the courts.**

**EVANS:** It would be difficult. In the Soviet Union, for example, they don't consider somebody an alcoholic until they have health problems. We would consider that person a chronic, late-stage alcoholic. They don't define it as alcoholism until it is a chronic, final-stage problem.

**DREWS: What about in England?**

**EVANS:** They also lag behind the U.S. in alcoholism recognition and treatment. In England, the government has alcoholism clinics that try to teach people how to drink. They're just now starting to use 12-step programs.

Holland has a very good clinic in Amsterdam called the Jellinek clinic. They use 12-step methods there. I've seen them develop over the years. Initially, they were just psychiatrically-oriented, but now, you see the 12 Steps of A.A. on posters all over the walls.

Internationally, treatment is getting better, but it's slow.

Mr. Evans is available to provide seminars and training on:

Alcoholism and family law
Alcoholism and domestic violence
Kids, drugs, and the law
Legal issues in treatment
Drug testing in employment, treatment, and criminal
    justice
Treatment, employment and confidentiality
How to use the law to help an alcoholic

David Evans also has a private law practice in New Jersey, specializing in alcoholism and the family, and other-drug-related issues. You may contact him at 35 Cold Soil Road, Lawrenceville, New Jersey 08648 or call him at 609-896-3923.

# Chapter Thirty-Two:
## Intervention

An intervention occurs when the family or employer or court system forces the alcoholic to go for help. This is usually done when there is "clout" — i.e., when there are consequences that you can "hold over the alcoholic's head" to make him or her choose treatment. The employer can say "get sober or lose your job." The court can say "go to treatment or lose your driver's license." The family can say "get sober or you lose us."

But before one can even think about intervention, sometimes families get confused by issues, like: Do you even have the right to say somebody is an alcoholic (much less demand that they do something about it)? Families sometimes ask this after they hear someone in a family recovery program say that "no one has the right to call someone an alcoholic." Probably someone said that in a meeting years ago, and someone else took it for gospel because they heard it. (Although this is not part of written official 12-step literature — it's just "lore" that's gotten some validity because it was said so often — it got passed down because it sounded good.)

But what does it mean? It means that if you say no one has the right to "call you" an alcoholic — then, in your gut, you feel it is a name-calling.

Alcoholism is either a disease or it isn't. There may be a stigma about it, but we just contribute to the stigma by saying we can't "call someone" an alcoholic. How come I can Call Someone a diabetic? *Do* you believe alcoholism is a disease — or don't you?

(You know, it's amazing: we can plan to leave a marriage for the effects of a spouse's alcoholism on us — but then we hear that we can't say that we're planning to leave for the reason that we're planning to leave?! What do we say, "I can't name what you have, but I'm leaving you for it?!")

Deep in our guts, it's very hard to believe it's a disease; but if we don't break the shame, the silence — we continue the stigma.

Now, it's true that in the final analysis, the only diagnosis that will keep a person in treatment is self-diagnosis — but hearing from others that one has the disease can sure help crack through one's own initial denial!

One more thing: some people also think that we shouldn't attempt to do an intervention because it gets families more embroiled with the disease process — and the aim of family recovery is to get less involved with the disease: to detach from it.

Yes, the aim is to get detached from the effects of the alcoholism. We *can* do this by acting the way Employee Assistance Programs do at job sites: We can do an intervention, but decide not to revolve our lives around whether the alcoholic will finally choose treatment. We can do the intervention, and know then, that we have tried everything.

And then we can let go of the results. Let go and let God.

I suggest that if you do an intervention, go to a movie, afterwards. Try to get your mind off of it. Let the results go. You have done all you can. That's all anyone can do.

\* \* \*

## Interview with Robert K. White, President, National Council on Alcoholism and Drug Dependence, Maryland Chapter, and professional interventionist for eleven years:

**WHITE:** There's usually at least an 80% success rate in interventions, if there are consequences attached, such as: the family is ready to do something significant, like the spouse is ready to separate or divorce; or the adult children are ready to withdraw their support until the person seeks treatment; or there is a job on the line. Those kinds of interventions tend to be more successful in getting the person to agree to treatment.

**DREWS: When you say adult children withdrawing their support — what kind of support?**

**WHITE:** They might say they're not going to have the parent over to family functions until he seeks appropriate treatment. Or they're not going to bring the grandchildren around until their mother or father is sober, because they don't want the children to see them that way.

DREWS: If one of the adult children is ready to do an intervention — and if other family members are in family treatment, but just too scared as yet to do an intervention — I think it's important that the adult child who's ready to intervene not punish the rest of the family for not being yet ready to do anything — not stop *them* from seeing the grandchildren.

WHITE: Right. Each family member needs to respect the other family members where they are.

DREWS: I don't insist that people have to *feel* loving to have an intervention. And they don't have to feel guilty because they don't feel loving. The *process* is a loving thing, even if you don't feel loving, because it is a very positive thing to help somebody into treatment.

WHITE: That's right. But there's no room for anger in the intervention itself. They can be angry and they can deal with that anger, but not during that hour of the intervention. And there's a very practical reason for this. *It's not to invalidate the family anger.* It's because the intervention is the place and time where you need to present the facts dispassionately. Objectively. Because showing a lot of anger raises the alcoholic's defenses. You need to present your information objectively so you can get in *under* their defenses.

DREWS: You want to take away the alcoholic's defenses so that he or she has fewer defenses against what the interventionist is saying. So, it's really very practical! It's not a moral issue that you can't show anger during that hour. It's a tactical question!

\* \* \*

DREWS: I hear this all the time: "My husband is too smart for an intervention. He'll run circles around you." It doesn't seem to matter what the alcoholic's education is or what he or she does for a living. The family always thinks the alcoholic is smarter than he is. They don't really believe that it's the *alcoholism* that's cunning and powerful. They think it's the *alcoholic* who's cunning and powerful. What's your experience in this?

WHITE: If you have an alcoholic who's a high-powered professional, what helps is to have an expert there, who is able to go eye-to-eye with the alcoholic. For example, with a physician, it's helpful to have other physicians there, when you're doing the intervention. Physicians who are knowledgeable about alcoholism. At least one physician that the alcoholic knows — or knows about — and respects! So that if there's a question of "you're not my peer," you bring in peers.

**DREWS: And that can also prevent the alcoholic from acting out with anger toward the family. He wants to impress this other doctor who's sitting there.**

WHITE: Right! But, in most cases, if the spouse is saying that the alcoholic's going to be too smart for the interventionist, she is too close to the problem to see it clearly. She has lived within the problem too long to see her alcoholic realistically.

**DREWS: She sees the alcoholic as more powerful than he is.**

WHITE: Yes! What the family member doesn't know is that in an intervention, she doesn't have to go one-on-one with her alcoholic husband in a debate about whether or not he has a problem. There's a group together who will do the intervention, so the group comes in with strength. They rehearse it all ahead of time, privately.

\* \* \*

**DREWS: At the intervention itself, the professional interventionist and the people who are going to be in the intervention have gathered together. Who makes the alcoholic show up at that time?**

WHITE: If you told the alcoholic ahead of time that he was coming to an intervention, he wouldn't come. So it is usually arranged that the meeting will take place when you know the alcoholic will be at a certain place at a certain time, when he probably won't be drinking — for instance, at 7 a.m. at his or her house.

**DREWS: What happens, at that point?**

WHITE: Most of the work of the intervention has taken place before you get to the intervention itself. It happens in the two or three sessions beforehand when the family gets educated, trained, and rehearses what they're going to say. Without the alcoholic present. That's where they get organized. And they get a sense of confidence because they've rehearsed it. They know exactly what they're going to say and they have a plan for each kind of outcome.

\* \* \*

**DREWS: What if the alcoholic says, "I'll go to A.A. I'll go every night. I'll do 90 meetings in 90 days. But I won't go to a treatment center."**

**WHITE:** Some people will say, "I can do this on my own." Or they'll say, "I can do this by stopping drinking and going to A.A. meetings without going to treatment." Many times you're left with a situation where you say, "Okay, we'll try it your way, and if it works that's fine. But if it doesn't work, the first time you pick up a drink, you'll try it our way." That's called a contingency plan.

**DREWS: Suppose, to get you out of his house, he says, "Okay, okay." What guarantee do you have that there will be any follow-through?**

**WHITE:** That's where consequences have to come in. That's where each family member has to decide, "Well, if this person does not seek appropriate treatment at some point, what is it I'm going to do, or not do, as a result of that?"

And, sometimes the family member may feel there is nothing he's going to do. Sometimes, the family has an intervention without consequences offered, just to take this one shot at letting him know how they feel about the alcoholism.

**DREWS: They're just willing to go through with it, to have an organized, thorough, professional discussion about the alcoholism.**

**WHITE:** Yes! It is still worth it to do the intervention because it's a very powerful thing to do. And even if the alcoholic doesn't go to treatment that day, it's made quite an impression.

**DREWS: You've cracked through a lot of the alcoholic's denial. Because during the process, a lot of the alcoholic's typical denial statements are exposed for what they are. Give us some examples of that, please.**

**WHITE:** The alcoholic will say things like, "Well, okay, people here are all telling me I have a problem with alcohol. I must have a problem, but I can stop on my own. And I don't need anybody's help." Then, we try to help them see what their experience has been in the past, of trying to do it themselves. Of how it hasn't worked.

**DREWS: Does that usually work?**

**WHITE:** Yes, if the family members have some good examples of how he's tried to stop drinking. Like, "In 1984, 1985, 1986, 1987, and 1988, you've said you'd stop drinking. You've tried that before. You tried even cutting down in the past. It never lasted more than a couple of days."

The professional facilitator makes sure things stay on track; offers some confrontation to the alcoholic if he is in denial; and leads the group through the process.

**DREWS: What if the family gets scared? What if the alcoholic starts glowering at them, giving them dirty looks, and they back off? Can the interventionist then usually calm the alcoholic down enough for him to listen?**

**WHITE:** Yes!

\* \* \*

**DREWS: Most alcoholics — once they get into treatment and start going to A.A., really get into it — lose that original bitterness they had towards the family for intervening. How long does that process take for the alcoholic to lose his anger about the intervention?**

**WHITE:** Well, first of all, many people are not mad about it in the first place. Many alcoholics come away from the intervention — even if they disagree with going to treatment — with such a sense of their family's love and caring, they wind up not mad at all.

But if they are angry, or if they feel like people have conspired behind their back — usually by the end of the treatment program, they've completely changed their mind about it, and are very grateful. Because they finally see how much people have cared enough to go to all this trouble. You need to get the alcohol and/or other drugs out of their system enough so they can see what the reality is.

\* \* \*

**DREWS: Is there any way to make this easier on the spouse — so she doesn't seem like the "bad guy" for organizing this intervention?**

**WHITE:** It's never just one person's idea. It's presented as a family, as a group, so that it doesn't come down to a "Well, it was your idea!" *And,* if the spouse is afraid she's going to be seen as the bad guy, she can have somebody else kick it off. Maybe there is an adult child that the alcoholic loves very much. Let the adult child "be the heavy."

**DREWS: Now, if you have no idea who should be involved in the intervention, that shouldn't stop you from calling the interventionist. Because at your first meeting, you can draw up a list**

with the interventionist and decide, together, who would be best to be invited to be part of the intervention.

WHITE: That's right. In fact, at the initial meeting, what I like to do is make a big list and include people who may not even wind up being in the intervention. But they might provide a lot of information about the alcoholism that no one even knew, before. You can decide on the final intervention team, later.

DREWS: And if you have some children who are too scared to be a part of the intervention team, they can be a part of the preparation! To give all kinds of information. But they don't have to be a part of the actual intervention.

WHITE: That's right. And the preparatory meetings help to convince the whole family that there really is alcoholism! It helps to convince some of the family members who don't think there's any alcoholism in the family. There is *so* much to be gained in *family* recovery, just by going through the process!

Even if the alcoholic doesn't go to treatment, the family gets better.

DREWS: And with a professional interventionist, resistant family members will often begin to hear the facts — even if they wouldn't listen to them before.

WHITE: You might have a key family member who wasn't fully convinced there was a real alcoholic problem, until after she's heard everything that this professionally-led group had to say.

\* \* \*

DREWS: Now, about who to get to facilitate the intervention: a) The employer can do it if there is an Employee Assistance Program on the job. b) The family can get a treatment center to do it free — if it is an inpatient treatment center. They usually have an interventionist on staff who will do it. c) A family can get in touch with somebody like yourself — who is a freelance interventionist. In that case, the family would pay for that person's services themselves.

WHITE: If the alcoholic works at a place with an Employee Assistance Program, the EAP can do an intervention and the family can give the EAP counselor helpful information that would allow them to do an intervention on the job. Now, because of legal confidentiality, the employer can't tell the family anything — but the family can say anything they want to, to the employee assistance counselor, to help bolster the on-the-job intervention. And they can give that information confidentially. The employee assistance counselor cannot tell where they got that information. So the family is protected there.

* * *

**DREWS: How does a family member get in touch with you, and people like you, who are professional freelance interventionists, in different cities?**

**WHITE:** You can call the National Council on Alcoholism and Drug Dependence, at their toll-free number: 1-800-NCA-CALL. They have lists of interventionists around the country. And you can call me to do an intervention in the Maryland area, at my office number, which is: 410-328-8444.

# Part Six:
## Resources

# Books & Tapes by Toby Rice Drews
### (Please see other side of page for ordering information)

## BOOKS

**Getting Them Sober, Volume One** ........................ $9.95
Hundreds of ideas for sobriety and recovery; endorsed
by "Dear Abby" and Dr. Norman Vincent Peale.

**Getting Them Sober, Volume Two** ....................... $9.95
How the entire family acts; hundreds of healing ideas.

**Getting Them Sober, Volume Three** .................... $9.95
Dozens more ideas. Half the book is a special section:
"350 Diseases Resulting From Alcoholism."

**Getting Them Sober, Volume Four** ...................... $9.95

**Getting Your Children Sober** ........................... $9.95

**Get Rid of Anxiety and Stress** .......................... $9.95

**Sex And The Sober Alcoholic** ........................... $9.95

**Light This Day (Meditations)** ........................... $9.95

## AUDIOCASSETTES

**8-Audiocassette Album, "Counseling for Families of
Alcoholics"**
*Over 3½ hours of counseling help from Toby Rice Drews*

Topics include:

- Does marriage counseling help when one partner is actively
  drinking/other-drugging?
- When you feel guilty/crazy/enraged when they continue to deny
- Why 'we put up with it' and 'why we keep going back'
- Dryness vs. Sobriety
- When you feel depressed because you can't leave
- Intervention — how to make them go to treatment
- Adult children of alcoholics
- The charming alcoholic/addict and how they con the helping
  professionals
- much more

### regularly $80
### NOW for readers of this book: $39.95

### WITH PURCHASE OF THIS 8-AUDIOCASSETTE
### ALBUM, YOU WILL RECEIVE A FREE VIDEO:
### "GETTING THEM SOBER"

# Ordering Information
## for Toby Rice Drews Books and Tapes

**1.** Circle the items you want, on the previous page.

**2.** Please fill out the information below.

**3.** Tear out and mail this filled-out entire page (and your payment by check or money order) to:

**Recovery**
**P.O. Box 19910**
**Baltimore, Maryland 21211**

**4.** **✳✳✳ Please include $6.50 for shipping and handling.**

**PLEASE PRINT VERY CLEARLY:**

**Ship To:**

_____
Name

_____
Street Address

_____
City                         State          Zip

_____
Area Code and Phone

# Toby Rice Drews
## Is Available For:

## Counseling through long-distance telephone professional consultations

*Family members: call her for counseling help*

---
## (410) 243-8352
---

*

## Also Available:
## Semi-annual Retreats

*for families and health professionals.*

*Call Toby at above number for dates and information.*

# Become a Television Sponsor
## of the
# GETTING THEM SOBER SM
## television shows.

To feature your company or business, or to honor a loved one, and to help millions of suffering families and children at the same time, help us by becoming a TV-sponsor, and be featured in the rolling credits.

Aired nationwide and co-sponsored by local nonprofits who feature their phone numbers for immediate help for battered spouses and children and other victims of alcoholism.

---

All TV Sponsors will also be featured for an entire year **FREE** on the Getting Them Sober SM Internet site.

---

**For further information see the following page, or call Toby Drews:**

# (410) 243-8352

# 46% of American families have alcoholism.

The Getting Them Sober℠ Foundation is a new nonprofit charitable foundation created to help millions of these families begin to lose their fears and recover from the craziness of living with alcoholism.

We are producing half-hour TV shows for families of alcoholics about the issues that are in the *Getting Them Sober* books. We will give the shows out free all over the U.S., reaching tens of millions of spouses and children to help free them from the crazymaking and the abuse, and save many lives.

## *We need your help.*

Please send a donation. See the other side of this page for a form to tear out and send in. Or call Toby at **(410) 243-8352** for a free brochure.

Thanks,
Toby

Please fill out and tear off this page
and send in with your donation to the

# GETTING THEM SOBER℠ FOUNDATION

P.O. Box 50128
Baltimore, Maryland 21211

Enroll me in the foundation. I want to help other suffering families.

**Please check where appropriate:**

☐ A Friend ($5-$49)

☐ An Associate ($50-$99)

☐ A Sponsor ($100-$499)

☐ A Patron ($500-$4,999)

☐ A Benefactor ($5,000 plus)

☐ I want to be part of fundraising activities in my area. Send me more information.

| •501(c)(3) status applied for. |
| --- |

---

Your Name

---

Street Address

---

City                    State         Zip

---

Area Code and Phone

# Books Recommended by Toby Rice Drews

## *Healing and Joy-of-Living Titles*

available through your local bookstore

## Diary of Abuse/Diary of Healing
*by Jennifer J. Richardson, M.S.W.*

Secret journal of a child, from age 6 til adulthood, recording two decades of physical and sexual abuse, with detailed healing therapy sessions. A very raw and extraordinary book.

## Turning Your Teen Around:
### How A Couple Helped Their Troubled Son
### While Keeping Their Marriage Alive and Well
*by Betsy Tice White*

A doctor family's successful personal battle against teen-age drug use, with dozens of *powerfully* helpful tips for parents in pain. Describes the full gamut of emotions and healing of the entire family. Endorsed by John Palmer, NBC News.

# I See Myself Changing:
# A Meditation Journal
*by Linda Meyer, Ph.D.*

*Wonderful* weekly meditation book for all the teens/young adults in your life.

# Mountain Folk, Mountain Food:
## Down-Home Wisdom, Plain Tales, and
## Recipe Secrets from Appalachia
*by Betsy Tice White*

The joy of living as expressed in charming vignettes and mouth-watering regional foods! Endorsed by the TV host of "Great Country Inns" and by *Blue Ridge Magazine.*

# Wise Stuff About Relationships
*by Joseph L. Buccilli, Ph.D.*

A *gem* of a book; "an empowering spiritual workout." Endorsed by the vice president of the *Philadelphia Inquirer.*

# Eastern Shore Beckonings
*by John Pearson*

Marvelous trek back in time through charming villages and encounters with solid Chesapeake Bay folks.

# *If* you are concerned that a physician, nurse, dentist or attorney might be alcohol- or other-drug-impaired, you can:

1. Call the American Medical Association or the Nurse Licensing Agency, State Bar Association or State Dental Association in your area.

2. Ask for the person heading up the Committee for Impaired Professionals, or the Assistance Program for that profession.

3. Ask for complete confidentiality. They should assure it if you give information. As with any ideas, do this only if you are comfortable about it and if they will ensure your confidentiality.

4. They will investigate, quietly, to see if there is a job-performance problem. If so, they have the clout to insist on evaluation and treatment, if called for. They can pull a person's license, if need be, to use for pressure. It usually saves the life and the career of the impaired professional. And, of course, the impact for the public good is enormous.